Nacogdoches: Integration and Segregation,
Then and Now

Copyright ©2016 by Dawn Michelle Williams and Brandon L. Fox

All rights reserved. Printed in the United States of America. No part of this book may be used or reproduced in any manner whatsoever without writer permission except in the case of brief quotations in critical articles or reviews.

For more information:
Stephen F. Austin State University Press
P.O. Box 13007 SFA Station
Nacogdoches, Texas 75962
sfapress@sfasu.edu
www.sfasu.edu/sfapress

Book Design: Tinesha Mix
Cover Design: Tinesha Mix
Distrubted by Texas A&M Consortium
www.tamupress.com

LIBRARY OF CONGRESS CATALOGING-IN-PUBLICATION DATA
Williams, Dawn and Fox, Brandon
Nacogdoches: Integration and Segregation, Then and Now/Dawn Williams and Brandon Fox

ISBN: 978-1-62288-104-8

Nacogdoches: Integration and Segregation,
Then and Now

Edited by:
DAWN MICHELLE WILLIAMS AND BRANDON L. FOX

STEPHEN F. AUSTIN STATE UNIVERSITY PRESS
NACOGDOCHES, TEXAS
2016

TABLE OF CONTENTS

Introduction 7
    – *Dr. Jerry L. Williams*

Cultural Trauma and Social Inequality in South Texas 11
    – *Dr. Jerry L. Williams*

Los Adaes: The Fugitive Safe House 22
    – *Rolonda Teal*

A Case Study from Early Nacogdoches: Bernardo and Raphael D'Ortolan 30
    – *Dr. Tom Middlebrook*

East Texas: Fom Post Civil Rights to the Obama Era 41
    – *Dr. Dianne Dentice*

The Changing Racial and Hispanic Composition of Nacogdoches and Its Educational Institutions 48
    – *Dr. Robert F. Szafran*

Integration and Re-segregation: Voices from the Past and Present 67
    – *Dr. D. Michelle Williams*

Paradise Lost 74
    – *Dr. Osaro E. Airen, Justin Ikpo, Kim Foli,*
    & Alisha Hall

My Story: Experiencing the Racial Environment of the 60s and 70s in Nacogdoches, Texas 83
    – *Verdis Daniels*

I Have a Voice, So Listen! 91
    – *Brooke La'Shun Taylor-Johnson,*
    Dr. Brandon L. Fox, and Dr. Patrick S. De Walt

Social Injustice in East Texas: A Social Work Perspective 109
    – *Dr. Emmerentie Oliphant and David Mitchell*

Confessing Whiteness 117
    – *Rev. Kyle Childress*

Contributor's Page 122

NACOGDOCHES: Integration and Segregation, Then and Now

Introduction

It is December in Nacogdoches. Heavy fog hangs in the air leaving a wet film on the redbrick streets. Christmas decorations adorn the Convention and Visitor's Bureau and most of the business windows of Main Street, the northern boundary of Plaza Principal. A public square originally set out by Spanish colonists in the 18th century, the Plaza was located on the El Camino Real de los Tejas, a Spanish colonial road stretching from Los Adaes in what is now Louisiana to Mexico City. Over its three-hundred-year history, Main Street has experienced a great deal of change. So too, have the people who have called Nacogdoches home. Once the subjects of colonial powers (Spain and Mexico), then citizens of the Republic of Texas, and now citizens of the United States; local people have variously walked, ridden horses, and driven automobiles on these now mostly quiet streets.

As is the case with all cities, the constructed environment of roads and buildings reflect the desires and esthetics of those who have the power and money to build them. Often forgotten are those who have lived and continue to live on the margins of power. Their histories are harder to find in the cityscape of Nacogdoches though their contributions are undeniable. In large part, the forced labor of enslaved people created the early wealth of Nacogdoches and of the United States. Much of what Nacogdoches is today is a consequence of that time and the period of segregation that followed it. To see the legacy of those on the margins of power, one must leave the brick streets of downtown. This is so because for most of the the history of Main Street a Black person could not legally own property.

Located a few blocks from Plaza Principal, the Zion Hill and Shawnee Street neighborhoods are obvious remnants of the segregated history of Nacogdoches. So, too, is E. J. Campbell School, an African American School, from which many local African American residents graduated and still hold fond memories. While much reduced in size, these neighborhoods do give a sense of what life would have been like during segregation. What is not apparent, however, is the sense of community and belonging former residents report feeling in spite of how unequal their objective conditions certainly were.

Little Zion Church, an African American Church in the Historically Segregated Shawnee Neighborhood.

The remnants of Nacogdoches' segregated past are, however, not simply artifacts, they also are evidence that the social relationships of segregation are still persistently part of life in Nacogdoches today. To say that Nacogdoches is an integrated city is to miss the obvious fact that, while no longer legally segregated, the city remains practically segregated – residential neighborhoods, schools, and churches are evidence. This is a curious fact. Many White Americans believe racial division to be a part of the American past, a problem solved in the Civil Rights struggle of the 1960s. In part, this belief is fueled by an enviable optimism that our democratic system has finally lived up to its promise that all "men are created equal." In the later half of the 20th century, we hoped that our centuries long history of racial injustice was over. This belief, however, has a darker side. Some Americans came to believe that this new era of equal rights meant equal opportunity for all Americans and that we had entered a new "color blind" period of American History. This color blindness, it was thought, was not so much a consequence of changing social attitudes about race, but rather the fact that racial discrimination was prohibited by law, and therefore, race should no longer be an issue for public discussion. In the end, the perceived objective reality of civil rights laws became for some an alibi or excuse for not reconsidering private and subjective beliefs about race. Under the cover of legislated racial equality, pernicious racism, and discrimination persisted.

Zion Hill Neighborhood, Historically Segregated African American Neighborhood

NACOGDOCHES: Integration and Segregation, Then and Now

In spite of this often willful blindness about race, over the last few years, public conversations about race have again uncovered the not so colorblind nature of American society. Social unrest in places like Ferguson, Missouri and Baltimore, Maryland over the high profile deaths of African Americans at the hands of police have placed race on center stage in the public mind. These protests make the case that "Black Lives Matter," a fact that some see as contradictory to the perceived colorblindness of post Civil Rights era America. As a result, some offer a counter claim – "all lives matter." This debate makes clear that—for some Americans—race should have little place in public conversation, little place in a land where discrimination is banned by law and where everyone has equal opportunity. This position, however, ignores that in 21st century America race still matters. Ferguson, Missouri has taught us that. So too, does the built environment of Nacogdoches. If we are willing to look and listen, the evidence for historic and current racism and discrimination is in plain view.

This book is an attempt to reflect upon and document the experiences of African Americans in Nacogdoches nearly 50 years after the integration of public schools. In the chapters that follow, we document experiences with the voices of researchers - sociologists, educators, and anthropologists. We also listen to those who have lived through integration, but also from those who where too young to experience segregation, and thus, only have their own experiences of growing up after the Civil Rights movement. The picture that arises from these essays provides a complicated snapshot of race in Nacogdoches. For those who lived in segregated Nacogdoches, we find not only stories of racial tension, but also some fond recollections of community life and of the educational system. Other writers take a more critical view of the past and the present. What all writers share, however, is the hope for a better common future for Nacogdoches, a future in which racism and discrimination can truly be a part of our collective past.

The Beal Gym, a sign inside the front door dedicates the building to the "white children of Nacogdoches."

Cultural Trauma and Social Inequality in South Texas

By: Dr. Jerry Williams

Introduction

I confess to being an outsider in East Texas. I came here in 1998 fresh from graduate school in Kansas where five years earlier I had moved from Eastern Oregon, the place I was born. Over the last fifteen years I have seen the system of racial inequality in Nacogdoches with the eyes of a stranger in a strange land. This is not to say that racial inequality does not exist in Oregon or other parts of the country, only in Texas it seems more apparent and tangible. As strange as the racial system in south Texas seems to me, it cannot measure up to the sense of strangeness enslaved people brought here from Africa must have felt during the 18th and 19th centuries. From the oldest cultures on earth, these people must have felt dislocation and loss on a scale I cannot imagine. All these years later this loss still hangs heavy in the air in Nacogdoches. If you pay attention, the signs of slavery and segregation are everywhere.

Nacogdoches is a small town situated in the pine forests of southeast Texas. Its curious name is derived from the Caddo Indian language and means "place of places." First settled by native people more than 10,000 years ago, Spanish colonization began in 1716 with the building of the mission Nuestra Señora de Guadalupe de los Nacogdoches. Variously controlled by French, Spanish, and Mexican governments, the current feel of the city was put in place during the Republic of Texas (1836-1846). In those years Nacogdoches was a cotton frontier in the westward expansion of the forced labor system (slavery) from the Deep South. Following the Civil War Nacogdoches became, as did most towns in the south, a racially segregated Jim Crow community. Not until 1970 were Nacogdoches public schools integrated.

Much in the same way that Alfred Schutz (1964) contemplated the experience of the stranger, my experience as outsider in Nacogdoches has helped me to appreciate a curious truth. Those who grew up in Nacogdoches, both Black and White, often underestimate the extent of the present system of racial inequality and the legacy of slavery. There is something important and at least a little ironic about that. Those born in and growing up in this culture, any culture, come to equate "reality" in the larger sense with whatever cultural realities shaped their upbringing and life-long socialization. Phenomenologists call this sedimentation, the process by which everyday knowledge is accumulated and comes to be taken for granted (Berger, Berger, & Kellner, 1974). Put another way, in the course of our everyday lives we come to assume that what we "know" on a personal level is coextensive with what is "real and true." These truths, over time, obtain a substantial fixity, a givenness that for those who hold them provide an order making function. We get a sense for this when we find ourselves saying "that's just the way it is," or "of course" about some everyday "fact."

The taken for granted apprehension of reality as normal and non-problematic is at the heart of understanding the experience of African Americans in Nacogdoches. For humans, culture provides an order-making function. It is what allows us to experience the world as understandable, meaningful, and as having purpose. It is in the context of culture that we grow up, have a career, marry, have children, and eventually die. All such events "make sense" because we can rely on cultural meanings that we share with those around us and that have been passed down to us by our ancestors. However, for people of African descent living in Nacogdoches, the taken for granted chain of cultural meanings that would give life understandability has been systematically broken and rebroken over the last two centuries. In this respect, African Americans in the southern United States have suffered what I describe as cultural trauma. Cultural trauma refers to the abrupt and substantial rupture of culture, and therefore, its order making function. The major point I wish to make is that while current and past economic exploitation, racism, and discrimination are important explanations for the system of racial inequality in the South, we must also examine how cultural traumas such as the slave trade, emancipation, the plantation system, segregation, and then integration have helped to shape the current racial setting in Nacogdoches.

In what follows, I first examine the objective state of racial inequality in Nacogdoches by examining existing data about housing, poverty, and income. Next, I set out a theory of cultural trauma grounded in the phenomenological writings of Alfred Schutz, and the social constructionism of Berger and Luckmann. In the final section, I conclude by offering observations about how a theory of cultural trauma can add to the national debate about racial inequality and about how such an understanding can help shape social policy concerning race and the remediation of racial inequality in the United States.

Evidence of Racial Disparity

Documenting the system of racial inequality in Nacogdoches is not as complicated as it first appears. To do so we must find objective evidence that the experience of African Americans differs from that of the White population in objective and measurable ways. Indeed, when we look at the evidence, even forty years after integration it is very clear that profound differences do exist. Currently 58.5% of people living in the city of Nacogdoches are White, 28.8% are African American, and 18.8% are Hispanic (Census, 2010). Of the White population 21.8% live below the official U.S. poverty line (American Community Survey, 2009-2013). However, 41.7% of African Americans live below the poverty line, a rate nearly twice that of White residents. The racial disparity in income is similarly dramatic. Of White income earners in Nacogdoches 25.3% of households earned less than $20,000 per year; 38.9% of African American households did so (American Community Survey, 2009-2013). On the other end of the spectrum 6.6% of White households earned $150,000 per year or more while no African American Households had income of $150,000 or more (American Community Survey 2009-2013). Housing patterns also demonstrate that African Americans have a quite different experience in Nacogdoches than the White population. A quick drive around the city clearly shows that much of the city remains quite racially segregated. In fact, in the average White neighborhood in Nacogdoches only 14.5% of residents are African American (Census, 2015).

As is the case with the United States as a whole, the system of racial inequality in Nacogdoches is also evident in variety of other social issues. For example, as compared to Whites, African Americans on average obtain less education, are incarcerated at substantially higher rate, and more often victims of violent crime. Some of these differentials can be directly explained by current and historical discrimination (racial profiling, employment discrimination, separate and unequal school systems). However, to understand the depth of these problems we must see them not as individual problems resulting from the decisions of individuals, but rather as problems inherent to the social system itself, a system as we will soon discuss that has been dramatically shaped by cultural trauma. Before heading in that direction, however, it is important understand the nature of individualistic explanations for the racial divide in social problems.

Individualistic Explanations

In the United States many argue that differentials in income, poverty, and housing point not to social structures of inequality but rather to differences in education or to sub cultural differences. In a 2001 survey of 2000 people conducted by National Public Radio (NPR, 2001), the Kaiser Family Foundation, and Harvard University's Kennedy School researchers asked "which is the bigger cause of poverty today: that people are not doing enough to help themselves out of poverty, or that circumstances beyond their control cause them to be poor?" Respondents were nearly equally divided about this issue (48% said "people not doing enough" and 43% said "circumstances") This requires closer examination.

Arguments that racial and economic inequalities such as the ones just discussed are individual matters not products of social circumstances make two important assumptions. First, they assume that social disparities are representations of individual merit and effort - those who work hard and make the right choices do well, and those who make poor choices do poorly. Second, they assume that racism and discrimination are phenomena of the past not the present - that all Americans are born onto a level playing field where everyone has an equal opportunity for success. On closer inspection it seems that both assumptions are unsupportable. Racism and discrimination, while perhaps reduced, are ever present features of the modern American experience. So, too, is the generational nature of poverty. Poverty begets poverty and wealth more wealth. To blame current social disparities such as poverty and income upon individual characteristics is to "blame the victim."

As an aside, it is important to note that in the southern United States social disparities and other social problems are quite commonly viewed in individualistic ways. Peter Berger (1963) discussed the origin of this perspective when he pointed to the historical connection between "Bible Belt" religion and what he calls the discrimination and prejudice of the Old South, what he labels "The Black Belt." Making a historical connection, he argued that southern religion became distinctly isolated prior to the Civil War because it had quite openly supported slavery and the oppression of Blacks. Due in part to this isolation, southern religion took on an overly individualized and moralistic shape that construed "sin" as sex, drinking, gambling, and other species of moral failure. Absent from the southern conception of sin was any mention of social justice, or corporate sin, such as the Atlantic slave trade, or the enslavement of other human beings. As a result, Berger argues, southern religion became a "latent ideology" for slavery and later for segregation.

It is no wonder, then, that many in the southern United States resort to individualistic, victim blaming explanations for racial and social disparities such as exist in Nacogdoches. Such matters do not fall in the narrow scope of what is thought of as an appropriate concern for someone immersed in Bible belt religion. While most southern churches no longer openly support discrimination, they nevertheless have retained the narrow focus of earlier years therefore reducing social issues like poverty, unemployment, and discrimination to individual, moral issues.[1] This individualistic approach has an additional consequence. The result of seeing social inequality as consequence of individual choices is that these circumstances are viewed in a robustly ahistorical fashion. For example, poverty among African Americans is not seen as resulting from historical circumstances, but rather from the choices of individuals currently living.

In 2002 the Southern Baptist Convention apologized for racism and discrimination making the following statement:

> Be it further RESOLVED, That we apologize to all African-Americans for condoning and/or perpetuating individual and systemic racism in our lifetime; and we genuinely repent of racism of which we have been guilty, whether consciously or unconsciously...

It is obvious that the Southern Baptist Convention Baptist Convention made a particular effort to not apologize for past injustices. This is understandable given the individualistic focus of southern churches. If sin and morality are only matters of personal conscience, rather than past incidences of discrimination are not a matter of individual concern even if they have directly benefited or hurt those living in the present. In such a radically individualistic world only the present matters.

A Theory of Culture

In order to make progress toward a theory of cultural trauma that might help us to better understand the system of racial inequality in Nacogdoches, we must first understand what culture is and why trauma should be considered in this context. Culture is best defined as the pattern for group life. This is true in two interrelated senses. First, culture provides the rules by which we engage in social interactions. These rules range from the merely implied for example passing a stranger on the street to the explicitly stated for example paying taxes. Second, culture also provides us with cognitive patterns or recipes for what we think, feel, believe, and value. The most important attribute of the cultural pattern is that it is taken for granted as self-evidently real. That is, what I think and do takes on an unproblematic, "that's just the way things are" mentality. For example, in the United States a large percent of the

---

[1] It is important to note that not all southern churches have disavowed racist doctrine. Appleby Baptist Church in Northern Nacogdoches County openly professes racist beliefs.

population marries in monogamous relationships and wholeheartedly embrace democracy, not because these concepts are unproblematic, but rather because their meanings have been passed down to us as unquestionable. Culture, then, provides order to the inherently disordered human world.

Extending the work of Arnold Gehlen (1988), Berger and Luckmann (1963) argued that humans exist in a state of "world-openness." Born with little instinct, humans are presented with a world that is not predefined. "Lower animals" on the other hand, live in a world largely without choices; they do what they do because they follow a pattern set down for them in their genes. The human world is one of possibility as compared to that of the so-called "lower animals." This possibility, however, is not without cost. As mentioned earlier, world-openness exposes humans to anomie on a grand scale. A world without instinct is a world of potential chaos. Life as we know it would not be possible without some way to limit or restrict world-openness. Berger and Luckmann (1966) suggested that in order to do this we collaboratively construct social institutions. Social institutions are created in three stages or moments: habit, mutual typification, and institutionalization.

The first step in constructing social institutions is habit. Confronted with a bewildering number of choices, humans form habits that allow them to take an unthinking approach to daily life. Habit is repetition that allows us not to think, that is, to take the world for granted. We simply do what we have always done. Close examination reveals that, in fact, most of our daily affairs are simply strings of habits. In this first step of institution building world-openness is certainly limited. Habit is not altogether effective, however. World-openness remains a possibility because we not only can change prior habits; we also remember that our habits are products of our prior choices. Therefore, just as we have created habits, we can also change them. The next stage of institutionalization, however, further limits world-openness because it happens when our individual habits are carried out in respect to others. This stage is distinguished by what is called mutual typification.

Mutual typification occurs when our habits are pursued in the presence of others who pursue their own. This is to say our habits are mutually reinforcing. Berger and Luckmann (1966) characterized the mindset associated with mutual typification as "here we go again." Mutual typification is important because it provides a more durable sense of taken for grantedness than does habit. Alone I can change my habits. In the presence of others it becomes much more difficult to do so. Most often we just do what others expect us to do. However, mutual typification is not a perfect answer for world-openness. Even while performing our mutually typified habits, we nevertheless upon introspection, can recall that our habits were once choices, and that as such, other choices are (were) possible. It is not until the next step of the institutional process that world-openness finds its most effective remedy. This stage is institutionalization.

Institutionalization provides a profound sense of taken for grantedness, and therefore, the most effective antidote to the precarious position of world-openness. Following habit and mutual typification, institutionalization occurs when people are born into an already existing social situation, when subsequent generations are socialized in the context of existing mutually typified behavior. Because children know no other reality, the present state of affairs becomes taken for granted as "just the way it is." Berger and Luckmann (1966) characterized this mindset with the statement "that's just the way those things are done" (p. 59) They describe institutionalization in the following way:

> The objectivity of the institutional world "thickens" and "hardens" not only for the children but (by a mirror effect) for the parents as well. The "there we go again" now becomes "this is how these things are done". A world so regarded attains a firmness in consciousness; it becomes real in an ever more massive way and it can no longer be changed so readily... It becomes the world.... The parentally transmitted world is not fully transparent.... It confronts them as a given reality that, like nature, is opaque in places at least (p. 59).

It is important to point out that this last step is substantially more able to limit world-openness than the first two because subsequent generations do not have direct knowledge that the existing social order was constructed, that is, "cooked up" by those who have come before. Social institutions, then, become nomic instrumentalities - the instruments of social order. To put all this differently, for social order to be obtained, the social habits of others must be transferred to those who follow without the knowledge that these habits were social constructions. True social institutions always appear on eye level to transcend their constructedness. They take on a degree of fixity which is crucial to their capacity to control human life, they acquire an objectivity which Berger and Luckmann compare to that of nature (Berger & Luckmann, 1966). The social world, then, takes on a reality that is "opaque" with respect to its constructedness (Berger & Luckmann, 1966).

Cultural Trauma

The prior discussion of the origin or culture and social institutions now allows us to consider why the cultural trauma experienced by African Americans has had such a devastating impact and continuing legacy. Cultural trauma is best defined as a sudden break or disruption of social institutions and social practices - to break "the pattern for group life." To be considered cultural trauma, Sztompka (2000) suggested four factors must be present:

1. The experienced change must be sudden and rapid.

2. The change must be radical, deep and comprehensive.

3. The change is perceived as imposed from outside.

4. The disruption is experienced as unexpected, surprising, and shocking. (p. 450)

Similarly, Eyerman (2002) suggested that in order to be designated as cultural trauma, and in contrast to individual trauma, the change must be laden with negative effect, represented as indelible, and regarded as threatening to a societies existence or violating one or more of it fundamental cultural presuppositions. Stamm, Stamm, Hudnall, and Higson-Smith (2003) argued, cultural trauma involves more that physical destruction or people, property, and landscapes such as might be seen in warfare or ethnic cleansing. It directly or indirectly attacks what constitutes culture, or which there are some essential yet vulnerable elements...(p. 95)

The existing literature about cultural trauma largely adopts the term as a metaphor derived from the notion that individuals who have experienced trauma later in life frequently suffer "post-traumatic stress disorder" or a related set of psychological effects. As a psychological phenomenon applying to individuals, these notions have little utility in application to social processes and outcomes. Social processes are never simply aggregations of individual experience. As Durkheim (1982) pointed out, society is a "reality sui generis" - a sum greater than parts. However, the abstract notion that trauma experienced by a group as rapid, comprehensive, imposed from outside, and unexpected can impact future cultural outcomes is important. It is precisely this sort of trauma that was experienced by African Americans over the course of the last 300 years.

African American cultural trauma began with the Atlantic slave trade to the new world. It is well known that the slave trade devastated many West African countries. People were stolen from their homes and villages in a very abrupt and violent manner. As the ancestral home of all living humans, African cultures were well established and institutionalized. Generation after generation, Africans from distinct cultures learned the ways of the past: marriage patterns, childrearing, religion, etc. and changed them in subtle ways as each generation passed. For people living in these cultures, culture was what we have called a nomic instrumentality. It is what provided them a sense of normality and order. These cultural institutions helped to keep at bay the inherent lack of human order we have called world openness.

As we have also seen, these cultural institutions obtained their most power in respect to limiting world openness when they were passed down from prior generations. This is so because people born into a social system know no other system. It is for them taken for granted that the cultural pattern is "real" and unquestionable. The Atlantic slave trade dramatically ruptured the cultural patterns of West Africa and in their place left broken villages and human cargo bound for the "new world." For those who survived the Atlantic passage the life of an enslaved person now took place in a dramatically different locale and in the presence of unimaginable cruelty. For the newly enslaved person there could be no resort to prior cultural patterns to make sense of these new experiences. This was a world in which old cultural recipes simply did not apply.

Most of us think of the forced labor system in the United States as relatively static. We imagine burning African villages, the holds of ships crammed full of human cargo, and finally the slave labor camps where enslaved people picked cotton and other such duties. What is often not recognized is that the forced labor system of the southern United States was dynamic, and that the lives of enslaved people were frequently disrupted. For example, families were often broken apart when enslavers died or went out of business. Baptist (2014) pointed out that the system itself changed over the course of United States' experience with forced labor. With the expansion of cotton production to newly "acquired" land to the west of the old south, the forced labor system expanded and became even more brutal.[1] Slavery was transformed into an industrialized process concurrently with the development of the textile industry in England. Such changes complicate the picture of cultural trauma considerably. Following the initial trauma created by enslavers in Africa, cultural trauma was recreated on a regular basis once in the new world. Not only had enslaved people lost their original cultural bearings, once they established new cultural protections against world openness, they too were regularly torn apart. Such devastations did not allow intact cultural forms to be passed

---

1   The western expansion of slavery was accomplished in no small part because millions of acres of land were stolen from the Creek, Cherokee, and other Indian peoples. The Indian Removal Act and the dislocation of indigenous cultures also created substantial cultural trauma.

down from generation to generation thus prohibiting social institutions to fully form and to be taken for granted. As a result, enslaved people must have been aware of tenuous nature of their cultural practices. Cultural practices provide the strongest order making function when individuals grow up with them and are unaware of their origin and history. If not broken, culture has an anonymous character that makes it appear as not a social construction, but rather as something that just "is the way it is." When cultural practices are repeatedly recreated after trauma they lose this anonymous character until such time that they can be passed down from generation to generation in large part intact.

Cultural trauma did not end with abolition. The history of African Americans in the 19th and 20th centuries is one of continued cultural disruption, and therefore, trauma. Abolition and the resolution of the Civil War were no doubt historically positive developments for African Americans. However, abolition also provided a disruption of the tentative cultural institutions that had developed beforehand. This dramatic social change again threatened whatever sense of social order in place at the time. This should not be interpreted to say that the system of forced labor in the United States should have continued, only that its abolition created dramatic social change that threatened the sense of social order (no matter how perverse) enslaved people may have experienced before.

Following the Civil War and the period of reconstruction, a *de facto* system of slavery arose in the southern United States that we frequently refer to as the "plantation system." Erected upon the foundation of planter society and slave labor camps, the new system kept in place the servitude of African Americans with a share cropping system. Concurrent with this system across the segregated south that remained in place in Nacogdoches until integration in the Civil Rights period. No doubt, integration was an important and positive development in the southern United States. However, integration also caused substantial change and trauma to African American communities. In an interview given to the African American Oral History project Archie Rison discusses the dislocating effect of integration in Nacogdoches. He states,

> My high school, or let me put it like this, my community and high school was a very close knit, say, the community, sought after making sure that every child was [phone rings turns off phone] . . . I'll start over. The community was close knit, and there was a feeling of unity. One of the things I think that we noticed when integration set in was that this was loss. It was sort of a good and then a loss. We knew that integration was coming, but the unity of the community was lost to a certain extent.
> (African American History Project, 2010).

These comments demonstrate that while integration was on its face a positive development, it also carried with it some rather traumatic latent consequences.

The previous comments cannot do justice to the complicated history of slavery in the United States or the impacts emancipation, the plantation system, and integration had upon African Americans in Nacogdoches. However, when the rather insecure nature of human beings and the order-making function of culture are considered, historical events clearly can be shown to create a significant amount of cultural trauma, trauma that continues to this day.

Conclusion

The system of racial inequality in Nacogdoches cannot be denied. The economic outcome of African Americans and of Whites clearly illustrates this. I have argued that at least in part this disparity continues generation after generation because African Americans have experienced significant and ongoing cultural trauma. Current theories of cultural trauma do little to help us understand why trauma has such long lasting effects. The theory of cultural trauma presented here is built upon an understanding of culture that suggests no generation ever begins anew. Rather, each generation depends upon a sense of orderliness provided by a cultural foundation passed down by earlier generations. Within its bounds individuals find their lives understandable and predictable thus enabling them to pursue their plans and goals unworried by most daily concerns. As we have seen, the history of African Americans in Nacogdoches points out that cultural institutions that might have provided this sense of order were regularly broken. The resulting historical cultural trauma places African American communities at a profound disadvantage. In comparison, Whites have benefited from a rather continuous and unbroken cultural form. While White culture has changed over the years, it has nevertheless been passed down from generation to generation absent significant cultural trauma. Comparatively, therefore, its associated social institutions came to obtain a more continuous order making function.

Before concluding this conversation it is important to point out that cultural trauma and the anomie experienced by African Americans is only part of the picture. To fully understand the African American experience it must be understood that cultural trauma combined with important economic factors to expand the generational inequality between Whites and African Americans. Economic assets in any society are always finite in nature. Take for example, the case of land ownership. At the time of emancipation African Americans were thrust into an economic competition with Whites for land ownership. In the still agrarian south, land was the primary foundation of the economy. Of course, at the time of emancipation available land was already owned. If African Americans were to economically succeed they would need both capital and land. Of course, African Americans had neither. As a matter of historical fact they entered the economic competition late in the game and thus had no real chance to succeed. The same was true after integration. While integration theoretically leveled the economic and social playing field, it did not provide the resources (land and capital) for African Americans to compete for economic resources in any meaningful way. Combined with the legacy of cultural trauma, economic disadvantage was the only logical outcome for African Americans.

The realization that racial economic inequality results from long-standing economic realities combined with cultural trauma suggests that changing this system requires more than wishing it was different or educating people about racism. Healing cultural trauma will require an economic system that produces generational cultural stability. At present, the cultural trauma of the past is recreated daily throughout African American communities in the United States. Because of the absence of real economic possibility, these communities experience epidemic levels of violence, crime, and social problems. These difficulties are caused by and are the reflections of trauma from prior decades. That abuse is replicated across generations is not a new idea. In order to stop this multigenerational trauma, substantial effort must be made to create an economic base that provides real opportunities for African American communities. This will mean that economic resources must be redistributed. This is the only way social and economic parity can be gained.

Economic redistribution to reverse the trend of intergenerational trauma will be resisted by many in the White community on the grounds of fairness - "why should we pay for the wrongs committed by our ancestors during slavery and integration?" The reason is clear. In large part the wealth of the United States was built upon the institution of slavery. As Baptist (2014) pointed out in the time of slavery, most Americans outside of the south profited from slavery. The early infrastructure of the industrial north in large part owed its existence to slavery and the cotton trade. It also was a major source of investment profit for northern banks. In some way all White Americans today have economically benefited from slavery and the associated social order that has been part of the White experience. Redistribution, then, would address a historical unfairness that continues to work its way out in the lives of African Americans now living. The form such redistribution might take is beyond the scope of the present discussion. If progress toward racial reconciliation is to be made, however, economic redistribution must be a part of the national conversation.

References

African American Heritage Project (AAHP), (2010) East Texas African American Oral Histories, East Texas Research Center, retrieved from http://www.sfasu.edu/heritagecenter/422.asp.

Baptist, E. E. (2014) *The half has never been told: Slavery and the making of American capitalism*. New York, NY: Basic Books.

Berger, P. L. (1963) *Invitation to sociology: A humanistic perspective*. New York, NY: Doubleday.

Berger, P. L., & Luckman, T. (1966) *The social construction of reality; A treatise in the sociology of knowledge*. New York, NY: Doubleday.

Berger, P. L., Berger, B., & Kellner, H. (1974) The homeless mind; Modernization and consciousness. NY,: Vintage Books.

U.S. Census Bureau. (2015) Available from http://www.censusscope.org/index.html.

U.S. Census Bureau. (2010) Available from http://www.census.gov/2010census/. Durkheim (1892). [1895] *The rules of the sociological method*. Tr. by W.D. Halls. New York, NY: The Free Press.

Eyerman, R. (2002) *Cultural trauma: Slavery and the formation of African American identity*. Cambridge, MA: Cambridge.

Gehlen, A. (1988) *Man, his nature and place in the world, European perspectives*. New York, NY: Columbia University Press.

National Public Radio, NPR. (2001) Available from http://www.prb.org/Publications/Articles/2002/AmericanAttitudesAboutPovertyandthePoor.aspx.

Schutz, A. (1964) *The stranger.* Edited by Arvid Broderson, *Collected Papers II: Studies in Social Theory.* The Hague: Nijhoff.

American Community Survey, (2009-2013). Available from http://www.census.gov/acs/www/.

Stamm, B. H., Stamm, H. E., Hudnall, A. C., & Higson-Smith, C. (2003) Considering atheory of cultural trauma, and loss. *Journal of Loss and Trauma 9*(1), 89-111.

Sztompka, P. (2000) Cultural trauma: The other face of social change. *European Journal of Social Theory, 3*(4),449-466.

Los Adaes: The Fugitives Safe House

By: Rolonda Teal

Introduction

Louisiana historian Gwendolyn Midlo Hall clearly identifies the route from New Orleans to Natchitoches and then to Los Adaes as an 18th century route for enslaved people seeking freedom in her book *Africans in Colonial Louisiana*:

> Slaves escaping from New Orleans sometimes headed up the Mississippi River into the Red River and thence to Natchitoches, a French military post on the Red River near Spanish territory. Natchitoches to Adayes, a Spanish military post on the Red River in what is now Texas, was an established [slave] escape route.
> (Hall, 1995, p. 148)[1]

By 1721, "Adayes" consisted of a presidio and mission named after the Adaes Indians in the area. An earlier location of the mission, established in 1719, was re-located in 1721 when presidio Nuestra Señora del Pilar de los Adaes was added to prevent French westward expansion into Spanish Texas. The newly fortified site served as the capital of Spanish Texas from 1729-1770. Although Adaes was the capital of New Spain, it was not a self-sufficient society. Life was exceptionally hard for the soldiers and their families. Basic necessities such as food, clothing, and other materials necessary for survival were scarce (Galan, 2006). The inhabitants of the fort were threatened with starvation and as a result, they began trading illegally with French and enslaved Africans from Natchitoches, and Native Americans in the region. It was largely due to trading activities at Adaes that promoted the path between Natchitoches and the fort as an "established escape route".

Spanish officials ordered Los Adaes closed due to a lack of congregants at the mission and a poorly outfitted regiment of soldiers. By 1773, Antonio Gil Y'Barbo, a native resident of Los Adaes and subsequent founder of the town of Nacogdoches, led the people of Los

---

1   Los Adaes is not located on the Red River as stated by Hall in her book but is instead located on a road known today as El Camino Real de las Tejas.

Adaes along with others in the vicinity (approximately 300-500 people) to present-day San Antonio, Texas. In 1774, Y'Barbo and other Adaesanos left San Antonio and created a settlement on the Trinity River which they named Nuestra Senora del Pilar de Bucarreli. Occupied from 1774 to 1778, this site temporarily took the place of Los Adaes since it also had a church there, and "escaped slaves from Louisiana also arrived there" (L'Herisson, 1981, p. 42). In less than five years they abandoned this settlement due to raids by Natives, crop failure, and flooding (L'Herisson, 1981, p. 42). In 1779, residents moved again, this time to present-day Nacogdoches, Texas. As a result of the closing of Los Adaes and the subsequent closure of Bucarreli, freedom seekers reset their sights on Nacogdoches as a destination place in the attempt to acquire freedom. By 1800, Nacogdoches had become the second largest Spanish settlement in Texas. So why would freedom seekers choose Los Adaes as a destination? Why leave a slave owning French country for a slave owning Spanish country? There are three primary factors that led people of African descent to travel from as far away as New Orleans in search of protection and potential freedom at Adaes. First, the Spanish had prohibited the enslavement of New World populations after the initial exploration of the area. Second, a transportation corridor between Natchitoches and Los Adaes was already established which facilitated the exchange of food and merchandise between the two posts. Finally, there appears to have been a policy of returning captured freedom seekers only if they had committed a crime—otherwise, they were not returned.

Spanish Position Toward Slavery

The official Spanish position towards slavery was established in the late 1400s when Queen Isabella of Spain, in response to the second voyage of Christopher Columbus, decreed that New World peoples were subjects of the Spanish crown and should not be enslaved. After the second voyage to the New World, Columbus brought several enslaved Carib's back to Spain with him. Queen Isabella did not condone these actions and for the first time addressed the issue of slavery in her new territory. The issue actually pertained to enslavement of indigenous peoples and not particularly African slaves. However, since Isabella justified her position by declaring that the inhabitants of New Spain where now her subjects and should not be enslaved, one would assume it applied to all forms of slavery. Just a few years earlier in 1493, Pope Alexander VI, mandated that people in the New World be converted to Catholicism and prohibited their enslavement as long as they accepted Christianity. However, if the people reverted to their old religion then they could be enslaved (Hanke, 1949). Many colonists took advantage of the clause "did not convert" and used it to enslave indigenous people and subsequent Africans even though many of them never received formal instruction in Catholicism.

Throughout the New World territories, the attitudes of Queen Isabella and Pope Alexander VI were largely ignored and slavery began to blossom in portions of New Spain. However, that was not the case in all Spanish territories. At Los Adaes, which was in a borderland region, there were only two mentions of enslaved people being sold. Those sales involved Luis de Urrutia Cofre de Pazas to a resident from Mexico City while the other transaction occurred the following day and involved the sale of Antonio Nicolas Patricio Cafre de Passa to Manuel de Villanueva a citizen of Los Adaes (Garcia, 1748). Outside those two occurrences, the only other mentions of enslaved people at Adaes were in the context of exchanging trade items and seeking refuge.

The infrequent historical mentions of enslaved people at Adaes can largely be attributed to the borderland society associated with the mission and fort. The inability of the Spanish government to provide basic sustenance forced Adaeseño citizens, soldiers and their families who lived at Los Adaes, to perform roles not only as soldiers but also as farmers, cowboys, and laborers (Galán, 2006). Basically, the soldiers lived under impoverished conditions and as such could not afford slave labor. In fact, Adaeseño residents performed many of the daily activities, including physical labor typically reserved for slaves, including hiring themselves out to Frenchmen in Louisiana (Burton & Smith, 2008). This atmosphere led to a community whose physical environment was vacant of visible slavery as compared to French Natchitoches.

In addition to a lack of visible slavery, there also existed in this borderland region a "surprisingly inclusive society of Spanish residents" (Blyth, 2000, p. 8). When Marqués de Rubí made a report in 1767 after a military inspection of the presidio, he concluded that it was primarily "composed of people collectively fugitives from other provinces" (Galán, 2006, p. 223). The core group at the fort was as ethnically and culturally diverse as the freedom seekers who went there. A 1731 roster of soldiers with caste designations identified 60 men: 29 Español, 13 Mestizo, 9 Mulatto, 7 Coyote, 1 Indio, and 1 Lobo (Meacham, 2000). The soldier roster dates 30 years prior to the official report by Rubí. Yet it already indicated an atmosphere that was a direct contradiction to events in Louisiana and Spanish plantation colonies such as those in Puerto Rico and Cuba (Blyth, 2000). This virtually slave-free status continued in Texas territory as evidenced by a 1792 census of the region. Out of a total population of 3,005 residents there were 34 Negroes and 415 Mulattoes listed (Babcock & Cockram, 1792; Yoakum, 1855). No mention was made of slaves in the region almost 20 years after the closing of Los Adaes.

Los Adaes' unique position as a small Spanish colony with no need for enslaved laborers, helped in the assembly of ethnic and cultural groups in a relatively small area. In many documented cases of attempts at freedom, enslaved people followed the North Star in route to Canada or looked for quilts signs to tell them where to go next. Yet, freedom seekers from Louisiana are not known to have any of those celestial or man-made markers to help guide them as they traveled. Perhaps then, a freedom seeker's arrival at the mission and fort—with its diverse enclave of people—would instantly let them know they had reached New Spain and were on the correct path toward emancipation.

Once arriving at Adaes, the mission should have been one of the first places that a freedom seeker looked for. As previously mentioned, Spain's theological attitude regarding slavery focused on conversion of the person to Catholicism. If an individual was willing do that, then they should be free. Once inside the mission walls at Adaes, the freedom seeker should—at least theoretically—have received sanctuary. With the added benefits of the fort's location, the church had military protection should an irate slave owner try to forcibly recover an absent laborer. Los Adaes, because of the mission and fort combination, would have been a "safehouse" or temporary stop along the route as they sought interior Spanish regions such as Bexar, La Bahia, or Mexico City.

El Camino Real de los Tejas

A second reason freedom seekers sought Los Adaes was due to the existence of an established route into Spanish territory. Known today as El Camino Real de la Tejas, this route formed from a series of trails used by Caddo Natives for travel between villages. Spanish colonists used parts of those trails for the transportation of animals, military, civilian and religious personnel. Camino Real translates simply as the "Kings Highway" and continued to be used in this way throughout Spanish dominion. Louisiana citizens also used the road between Natchitoches and Adaes as a trade route and as a means of travel to interior regions of New Spain to conduct business. Due to its historical significance as a transportation route, El Camino Real is now part of the National Trails System and as defined by the National Park Service extends from Monclavia, Mexico to Natchitoches, Louisiana and covers approximately 2,500 miles in distance (National Park Service, 2011, p. i). (see Figure 1).

Figure 1. El Camino Real from Natchitoches, LA to Mexico as defined by the National Park Service (2011).

In terms of proximal distance, Los Adaes offered a haven for freedom seekers that could be reached within a day when traveling by foot from Natchitoches and sooner if traveling by horseback. For other enslaved people in the French regions, travel distances were greater, and it may have taken weeks or months to reach Adaes. This point is further illustrated through an incident that occurred in 1771. An enslaved woman Marie Anne, her son named Alexandre, a pregnant woman Charlot, and a male Louis had been gone for 18 months. Along the way they recruited other slaves. When arrested at the vacherie (cattle grazing land) of Louis Juchereau de St. Denis, former commandant at Natchitoches, they said they were headed for the Spanish fort of Los Adaes (Hall, 2006). This group of freedom seekers had come from New Orleans largely because of the fort's location along a well-known road leading into Spanish territory.

Another example of the use and importance of El Camino Real is illustrated in an enslaved man's trial for theft that occurred in 1757 in Natchitoches. During the interrogation of Etienne, it was revealed that his mother Marion sent him, "to Los Adaes to sell [some] cloth for silver" (Colonial Archives, 1757). Etienne also confirmed that his mother often sent hams to Los Adaes with a Spanish man named Maringouin who would bring her chocolate, silk, or small blocks of sugar in exchange for meat (Colonial Archives, 1757). The Spanish man Maringouin is likely Melchor Morain who served in the military at Los Adaes at various times between the periods of 1751 - 1762. This portion of the trial establishes that it was not uncommon for Natchitoches' enslaved to travel with relative ease to Los Adaes where they engaged in trade with Spanish residents.

The Etienne trial also establishes the existence of an escape network that existed between enslaved Africans from Natchitoches and Spanish citizens. As the trial proceedings continued, accusations of a conspiracy were revealed involving two Spanish military deserters, Miquel de la Cerda and Joseph Antonio de Acosita y Arias (Colonial Archives, 1757). Cerda and Acosta both served in the military at Los Adaes during the same period as Melchor Morain. Their interest in helping fugitives may have stemmed from Cerda's position as a Spanish deserter living in Natchitoches while Acosta's interest may have been is bicultural designation as being of both Spanish and African descent. Etienne volunteered that he had "conspired with all the slaves that they should go away" with the Spanish men to Los Adaes (Colonial Archives, 1757). When the hearing finally concluded several days later, 10 people were arrested on various charges. Four of the arrested were sent to New Orleans, including the Spanish deserter, Miquel de la Cerda. This trial represents one of the earliest documents from the region that illustrates Underground Railroad type activity between Spanish military deserters and Natchitoches enslaved. Apparently some Spanish citizens like Miquel tried to influence potential fugitives—especially from French Natchitoches—to take the road they were already familiar with in the hopes of walking to liberty.

When Los Adaes closed, the road that had led freedom seekers there, now became the same road that would lead them to Nacogdoches with the same aspirations. Fewer than a hundred miles apart, the trail from Los Adaes to Nacogdoches was the same one used by Spanish and French colonists, prior to that by Native Americans, and prior to that by buffalo. Thus the multifaceted historic significance of what is now El Camino Real de los Tejas National Historic Trail (see Figure 2).

Spanish Policy Regarding Captured Freedom Seekers

A third reason fugitives sought Adaes pertained to the 50-50 chance they had of obtaining liberty once they reached the site. By the late 1700s, French Louisiana restricted the freedoms of their enslaved population such as the ability to travel freely, engage in trade, and meet in groups (Burton & Smith, 2008). In addition, there was an increased presence of militia in the region during this period due to a fear of rebellions and escapes. These new policies towards the enslaved sometimes created tense situations for officials in both countries. There was a need by the French to maintain control over their enslaved population and be able to retrieve them from Spain in the event they should abscond. At the same time the Spanish had a need to maintain peaceful relationships with their French neighbors, especially those at

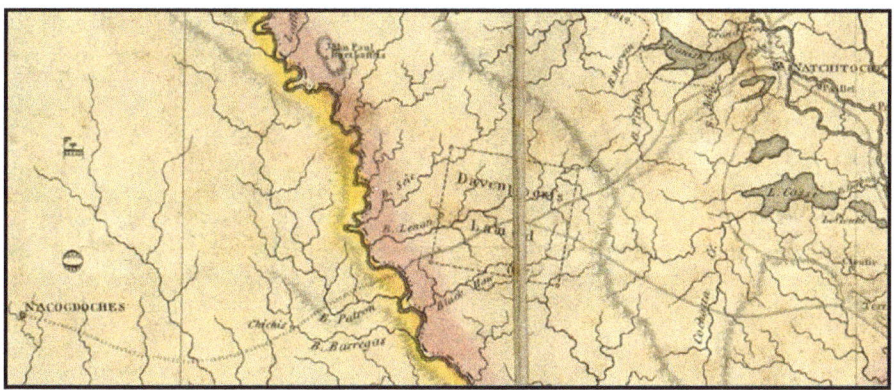

Figure 2: This map highlights the territory between Nacogdoches, TX and Natchitoches, LA. The main road connecting the two towns is El Camino Real (William Darby map, 1816).

Adaes, yet also be able to flex their muscles as a military entity for Spain. Consequently, when freedom seekers arrived at Adaes decisions were often made on an individual basis versus a standard policy.

An example of how those dynamics often played-out is observed in a letter dated September 24, 1768 in which Viceroy Marqués de Croix (Mexico City) informed Governor don Hugo Oconor (Texas) that a mulatto slave from New Orleans had sought refuge of immunity at the church at Los Adaes (Garcia, 1748). The new interim Governor Oconor unaware of how to handle freedom seekers awaited a response from his superiors on the matter since French officials had requested the return of the fugitive. When the viceroy did not receive a response in a timely manner, he returned the enslaved man to his owner (Croix, 1768). This case - exemplifies the general problems that faced Spanish government officials on how to handle the issue of fugitive slaves. Amarillas informed Oconor that he was aware of his doubts about returning the slave to Louisiana. However if the enslaved had not committed any crimes he was not to be returned to his owner. Yet, if the man left Louisiana because he had committed a crime, then return him. This, Oconor suggested, should be, the policy practiced in any similar future events (Garcia, 1748).

Unfortunately, there are not any known examples of freedom seekers who began their journey from some place in Louisiana, came to Los Adaes, and then went on to obtain freedom in an interior Spanish province. However, we should not expect to find examples of success stories. In fact, the importance of Adaes as a destination along an established escape route is best supported from the instances in which the freedom seekers failed. For it is in that context that we find correspondences between Spanish officials as they discuss slave policies. It is through the failed attempts that we find letters from French citizens demanding the return of their property. Those brave individuals who did make an attempt at sovereignty and were successful would not have shared that information for fear of being recaptured.

For those never recaptured, they either traveled into the interior regions of New Spain settling in places like San Antonio or southwest into Mexico or simply joined forces with local Native American tribes. Some, however, likely stayed in Nacogdoches and tried to make a life for themselves there. Arguably, the biggest draw to Nacogdoches was the promise of freedom. Shortly after the Louisiana Purchase on April 30, 1803, Spain, likely in retaliation towards the French, announced that any enslaved person who crossed the Sabine River would be free. As a result, people left Louisiana, Mississippi, and as far as Kentucky heading towards places like Nacogdoches, which would have been the first town they reached once across the Sabine River. It is noteworthy to mention that the escape plan from Natchitoches occurred only six months after the Spanish decree. By 1829, in an unprecedented move, Mexico's Vice President, Vicente Guerrero conditionally abolished slavery in all Mexican territories.

Summary and Final Remarks

It is clear that the settlement referred to as Los Adaes was perceived to be a destination of freedom for enslaved people in 18th century Louisiana. This perception is undoubtedly related to the fact that the Spanish Crown and religious authorities had prohibited the enslavement of peoples in the New World early in the Spanish occupation. Unfortunately, this prohibition was oftentimes ignored as economic necessity prevailed. Cattle-ranching was the primary economic pursuit for the Spanish in the area of Los Adaes, and since labor requirements for ranching are much less than for plantations, there were infrequent mentions of enslaved people in this part of the province of Texas.

Los Adaes was not self-sufficient, so trade continued between the French thus leading to a trade route between the two countries. This route, El Camino Real de los Tejas, was likely the route chosen by freedom seekers on their way to Los Adaes. Upon reaching Los Adaes, even if detained by Spanish authorities, there was a good chance that they would be allowed to continue on their journey if they had committed no crime. By the late 1700s, free people of African descent formed 15% of the population in Texas (Barr, 1996, p. 3). It is quite likely that some proportion of that 15% could be attributed to 18th century freedom seekers who came from Louisiana to Texas by way of Los Adaes and along El Camino Real de los Tejas. Once Adaes closed and the town of Nacogdoches formed, freedom seekers were given the promise of liberty if they made it past the Sabine River. Although some were still returned to their owners, once in Nacogdoches, we would be remiss if we did not acknowledge their bravery and boldness in the face of oppressive conditions.

References

Babcock, M. M., & Cockram, M. W. (1792, December 31). Census report of Nacogdoches [Transcribed]. Bejar Archives, 996-1001. In Prov.a de los Texas Jurisdion del Pueblo de ntra. Senora del Pilar de Nacogdoches. [Microfilm]. (Roll 22).

Barr, A. (1996). Black Texans: A history of African Americans in Texas, 1528-1995. Norman, OK: University of Oklahoma Press.

Blyth, L. R. (2000). Fugitives from servitude: American deserters and runaway slaves in Spanish Nacogdoches, 1803-1808. *East Texas Historical Journal, 38*(2), 6.

Burton, H. S., & Smith, F. T. (2008). *Colonial Natchitoches: A Creole community on the Louisiana-Texas frontier* (No. 29). College Station, TX: Texas A&M University Press.

Colonial Archives. (1757, July 12-13). Testimony in the complaint of Jean Fromentin [Trail proceedings]. In *Natchitoches Parish Clerk of Court Colonial Archives*. [Bound Conveyances]. (Vol. 1, Doc. 186)

Croix, M. (1768, September 24). Marqués de Croix to Governor Oconor of Texas [Letter]. In *Bexar Archives*, 0639,[Microfilm]. (Reel 10).

Galan, F. X. (2006). *Last soldiers, first pioneers: The Los Adaes border community on the Louisiana-Texas frontier, 1721-1779* (Unpublished doctoral dissertation). Southern Methodist University, Dallas, TX.

Garcia, F. (1748, September 7). Bill of Sale. In *Bexar Archives*, 1058. [Microfilm]. (Reel 8).

Hall, G. M. (1995). *Africans in colonial Louisiana: The development of Afro-Creole culture in the eighteenth century*. Baton Rouge, LA: LSU Press.

Hall, G. M. (2006). Afro-Louisiana history and genealogy, 1718–1820. Retrieved from *www.ibiblio.org/laslave*.

Hanke, L. (1949). *The Spanish struggle for justice in the conquest of America*. Dallas, TX: Southern Methodist University Press.

L'Herisson, L. E. (1981). *The evolution of the Texas Road and the subsequential settlement occupancy of the adjacent strip of northwestern Louisiana, 1528-1824* (Unpublished master's thesis). Louisiana State University, Baton Rouge, LA.

National Park Service (2011). *Comprehensive Management Plan/Environmental Assessment for El Camino Real de los Tejas*. National Trails Intermountain Region, Santa Fe, NM National Park Service, Department of the Interior. Retrieved from https://parkplanning.nps.gov/projectHome.cfm?projectID=12599

Rubi, M. (1767, September 14). Report on inspection of presidio los adaes. p. 3. In Archivo General de Indias-Guadalajara (1768) [Microfilm]. (Reel 4, Microfilm 114).

Yoakum, H. K. (1855). *History of Texas: From its first settlement in 1685 to its annexation to the United States in 1846*. Redfield, SD: Redfield Press.

A Case Study From Early Nacogodches:
Bernardo and Raphael D'Ortolan
By: Dr. Tom Middlebrook

While most of this volume focuses on the Black experience in Nacogdoches during the 40 years since integration, this chapter will glance back at racial relationships in our early local history. Prior to the century-plus of segregation following June 19, 1865, and even prior to the antebellum Anglo-dominated slavery practices that emerged in the 1830s, Nacogdoches was home to many people of African descent. Their stories are rarely told in local history books, and oral traditions from that time have all but vanished. This essay will illuminate the lives of two remarkable early Nacogdoches citizens from which the modern reader may draw parallels, or contrasts, to later social relations. The account presented here may enrich the historical context of the main focus of this book, and it may hint at some corrective understanding of long held assumptions about the past. In any event, this story will introduce an inspiring figure who is an unsung hero of Nacogdoches Black history.

Historical Background

Estevanico, a Spanish slave and a member of the ill-fated Pánfilo de Narváez expedition, is widely accepted as having been the first African person to set foot in Texas when he landed with two others on a raft near Galveston in the autumn of 1528. After being captured by coastal Natives, he escaped with his companions and Álvar Núñez Cabeza de Vaca and made his way to Mexico in 1535. He was killed in 1539 by Zuni Natives in western New Mexico (Chipman, 2010).

A century and a half later, East Texas became a dynamic cultural and political boundary between European adversaries, Spain and France. This rivalry played itself out in the heart of the "Kingdom of the Tejas," an alliance of Hasinai Caddo tribes in the Angelina-Neches river basins. Spanish claims to the region were challenged by three developments: 1) Robert Cavelier, Sieur de La Salle's small colony at Matagorda Bay in the mid-1680's, 2) the infiltration of French traders into East Texas, and 3) the establishment of a French post in 1714 at Natchitoches. Although the Spanish established two fragile, short-lived missions amongst the Caddo groups around 1690, their permanent presence in Texas began with the Domingo

Ramón Expedition in 1716 and the missions it founded. Among the 75 persons Ramon listed as members of his entourage was "Juan de la Concepcion" was probably the earliest person of African descent to walk into Nacogdoches. Other Afro-Mexicans accompanied Governor Alarcon on his re-supply of the East Texas missions in 1718. After a brief abandonment, the massive Aguayo Expedition of 1716 re-established six Franciscan missions in eastern Texas and placed two presidios to guard them. Again, persons of African descent were part of the expedition and lived at the Spanish outposts.

Presidio Los Adaes, founded in 1721 near present-day Robeline, Louisiana with its community of around 400 souls, became the capital of Texas for a half century. After the Treaty of Paris was signed in 1763, ceding Louisiana to Spain, there was little need to maintain the three remaining missions and Presidio Los Adaes. Consequently, these eastern outposts of New Spain were recalled to San Antonio in 1772 despite the vigorous protests of the *Adaeseños*. When they arrived in Bexar, they discovered that much of the best land had already been taken by Canary Island immigrants. After much pleading and a four-year miserable sojourn on the Trinity River at Bucareli, the *Adaeseños* finally returned to the pineywoods of East Texas in 1779 under the leadership of Antonio Gil Y'Barbo. There they established a town near the site of the old Zacatecan Mission Nuestra Señora de Guadalupe de los Nacogdoches. Over the next two decades, Nacogdoches became a leading trading center and the unofficial Spanish "gateway to Texas" from the east. Diverse groups of Caddo and newly arrived Immigrant Native American peoples, European and American settlers, and African persons, enslaved and freedmen, all traveled along the *El Camino Real de los Tejas* and stopped in Nacogdoches.

Into this dynamic social ferment, a colorful figure emerged in 1796 when Don Bernardo D'Ortolan arrived from Natchitoches with two sons and group of slaves. The remarkable story of this man and his slaves, living on a Spanish land grant/rancho ten miles west of Nacogdoches, is an important illustration of the cultural interplay of the times.

Bernardo D'Ortolan

Bernardo D'Ortolan was born August 2, 1750 in Parish St. Michel, Bordeaux, France, the son and grandson of commissioned French ship captains (Archives Municipales de Bordeaux, n.d, CG256, act. 1397). The date and nature of his passage to the New World are unknown, but he appears in Natchitoches Parish records in October, 1776 when he married Marie Anne Grappe, a woman from a prominent and wealthy local family (Burton & Smith, 2008, p. 39, 153; Mills, 1977, p. 1026). During the 12 years of marriage before her death, Marie Grappe D'Ortolan gave birth to four sons and a daughter (Mills, 1977, p. 1426, 1728, 1782, 1304, 1848, 1902). Records suggest that only two sons survived until adulthood. Bernardo D'Ortolan apparently inherited a group of slaves who had belonged to his first wife. D'Ortolan married again in July, 1793 to Catharina Bardon, but he became a widower a second time the following year (Mills, 1977, p. 3393; Blake, n.d., Supp. Vol. I, p. 140, 311). During the nearly 25 years he lived in Natchitoches, he became loyal to the Spanish crown and rose through the ranks of the military. Don Juan Maria de Ripperda, Governor of Texas, acknowledged D'Ortolan as a "faithful interpreter" with the Friendly Tribes in the "Royal Service" when he was still a young adult. He may have followed the command of Bernardo de Galvez against the British at Manchac, Baton Rouge, and other encounters (Susan Holley, personal communication). In 1778-79 he accompanied the De Mezieres expedition to Bexar (UTITCSA, 1975, p. 49). D'Ortolan was eventually promoted to the captain of the Spanish cavalry and militia.

Bernardo D'Ortolan was by nature an opportunist (Susan Holley, personal communication), seizing the chance to rise in the local military system and marrying into a wealthy family. Part of his personal economic opportunity was the ownership of slaves. The community of Natchitoches was likely the principal location of D'Ortolan's development of racial attitudes and behaviors. Understanding 18th Century Natchitoches social structure is important to D'Ortolan's story.

Following French practices in Canada, the first slaves in Natchitoches were Native Americans captured in battle or traded through other Indian groups, but by 1722 there were 20 West African slaves living in this community (Burton & Smith, 2008, p. 55). Over the next 40 years, the number of African slaves rose dramatically, reaching 239 by 1765 when the Spanish took control of the territory, despite a restriction on African imports after 1731. King Louis XIV's Code Noir of 1685 did little to protect the slaves in Natchitoches. Although the Spanish officially granted more rights to enslaved persons than the French, the Ordinance of 1770 in Natchitoches provided restrictions on slave assembly, free movement and ownership of items that could be used as weapons (Byrd, 2008, p. 72). While there was never much question about French creole hegemony in colonial Natchitoches, there was also clear evidence of intercultural and interracial relationships and marriage between European, African, and Native persons. The Spanish developed an elaborate caste system to keep track of the various permutations of racial and cultural genetics. There were increasing numbers of free persons of color during the Spanish era. Eighty-four manumissions were recorded in Natchitoches between 1774 and 1803. Although there were only 23 free persons of color during the French era in Natchitoches, there were 181 such *libres* by the early American period in 1810 or 6.3% of the total population (Burton & Smith, 2008, p. 92-94). As a young adult then, Bernardo D'Ortolan lived in rapidly evolving frontier colonial community that was racially complex, modestly integrated and maintained Native and African slavery with some nuances distinct from later Anglo practices.

In 1795, D'Ortolan became a controversial figure in what has been called the Natchitoches Revolt, an uprising among some of the French residents of Natchitoches against the ruling Spanish authority (Ocaruz, 1964). While he was traveling to Bexar to inform officials there of the unrest in Natchitoches, a group of four Frenchmen disguised as Indians and calling themselves the *Revenantes*, or "ghosts", attacked a group of French partygoers who were Spanish loyalists. The "ghosts" composed a ballad celebrating their intimidation of the Spanish sympathizers, and three of the stanzas made veiled threats toward D'Ortolan (Hatcher, 1926, p. 49-55).

No doubt because of his more tenuous position following the Natchitoches Revolt, D'Ortolan was transferred to Nacogdoches as Captain of the Militia in 1795-96 (Blake, n.d., Vol. XXXV, p. 272; Vol. IV, p. 94). He brought along two sons, Juan Baptiste, age 18, and Raymond, age 15, along with nine slaves that included a female, Maria Jauna, her five daughters and one son and two young adult males (UTITCSA, 1988, Vol. I, p. 290). D'Ortolan lived as a gentleman farmer and was involved in the administration of the Spanish military post.

D'Ortolan received a large land grant in October 1796, dubbed "Rancho San Bernardo del Loco" in western Nacogdoches County (Blake, n.d., Vol. XXX, p. 220). The 1809 Nacogdoches Census describes his holdings as a:

> Ranch – two log houses for residence; one that covers a grist mill; another for granary and two for his negroes, on land consisting of a league and a half front and the same in depth, granted by Lt. Dn. Jose Ma. Guadiana, on which he has a field and summer pastures; he has 26 horses and 26 head of cattle (UTITCSA, 1984, Vol. 2, p. 11).

The site of Don Bernardo D'Ortolan's rancho home is situated along the *El Camino Real de los Tejas* as illustrated on Juan Pedro Walker's 1806 map (see Figure 1). This corridor ran from Natchitoches through Nacogdoches, San Antonio and ultimately to Mexico City. It was a central transportation axis of Spanish Texas. It linked the diverse Texas population of the period, their trade, ideas and politics, and it connected their world on beyond to the American nation to the east. Bernardo D'Ortolan sold the northern portion of his grant to his friend and fellow French ex-patriot, Joseph De La Baume, around 1805.

Bernardo D'Ortolan and his sons are noted in the Nacogdoches census of 1797, 1798, 1799, 1804, 1805, 1806 and 1809 (UTITCSA, 1984, Vol. 1, p. 290, 308, 323, 368, 418, 425;

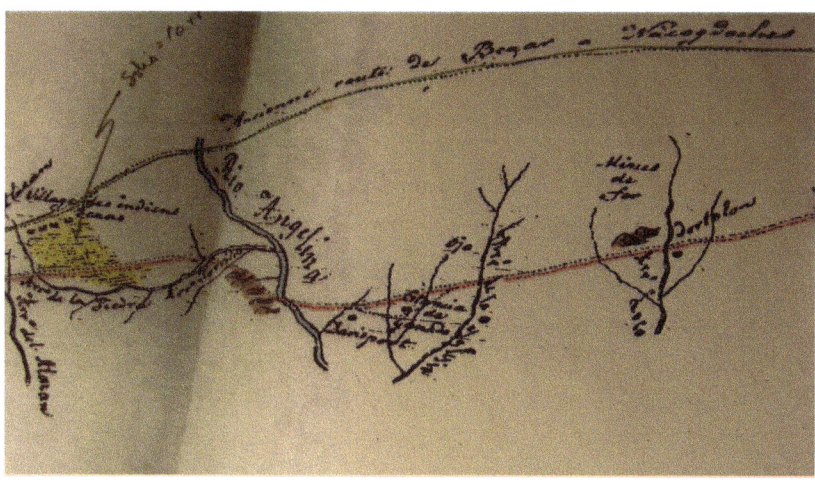

Figure 1. Juan Pedro Walker's 1806 map of El Camino Real showing D'Ortolan's rancho on right.

Vol 2, p. 11). The number, age, and gender of his slaves as recorded in the records varied over time. From 1797 until 1805, he was said to have between nine and twelve slaves; these numbers diminished to eight in 1806 and seven in 1809. Most of the slaves brought to Nacogdoches by D'Ortolan were children when he arrived. Seven of ten slaves were under 18 in 1798 while only four of eight were by 1806. Six of his nine slaves were female in 1797 while only two of his eight slaves were female in 1806. In summary, D'Ortolan owned fewer, older and more male slaves as time went on.

Perhaps typical of the times, Bernardo D'Ortolan's relationships with African enslaved persons were complex. As will become clear, this complexity may have been most striking in his relationship to a mature African creole woman slave named Maria Juana. D'Ortolan had married Marie Grappe in October 1776 who brought Maria Juana into their new home. Strikingly, both women had successive children in 1777, 1780 and 1782 just a few months apart. D'Ortolan may have been the father of some of Maria Juana's children. Notably, he saw to it that at least four of them were baptized in Natchitoches, but he listed "father unknown" in all cases on birth certificates (Mills, 1977, p. 2319, 2365, 2422, 2581).

Years later, after his move to Nacogdoches, D'Ortolan's relationships with his slaves were often contentious and negative. In late 1806, José Ramon, a 36-year-old African slave belonging to his close friend and neighbor, Joseph de la Baume, brought a lawsuit against Bernardo D'Ortolan (Blake, n.d., Supp. Vol. V, p. 362). It seems that José Ramon had fathered a child with 24-year-old María Francisca, a daughter of D'Ortolan's slave María Jauna. He petitioned the Spanish legal authority to allow him to buy the freedom of their child for 100 pesos. Both masters protested the lawsuit describing their slaves as "immoral", insubordinate, "incorrigible," and they wondered if the purchase money was stolen (Blake, n.d., Supp. Vol. V, p. 372-374). Ramon countered that he had saved money from the sale of crops and hogs he was allowed to raise on a plot that de la Baume had set aside for his use (Blake, n.d., Supp. Vol. V, p. 272-375). María Francisca slipped away from her home to help Ramon grow corn, beans, and sweet potatoes. D'Ortolan complained that the slaves sold "more pigs, more corn, and beans (at the Nacogdoches post) than I, who am their master" (Blake, n.d., Supp. Vol. V, p. 366). Ramon told the Spanish authority that he had been living with María Francisca for five years and had asked D'Ortolan several time for permission to marry her. The outcome of the lawsuit is unknown, although, years later in 1818, María Francisca, still enslaved to D'Ortolan, was noted in the baptismal records of Natchitoches to have given birth to a daughter named Marie Tecle, with a free male of African descent named Magsimino Juannot (Mills, 1980, p. 1073).

By 1804, María Juana was no longer living with Bernardo D'Ortolan. She may have gained her freedom by some means, but her departure appears to have been on bad terms. Bernardo complained in 1807 that he was "vexed" by his "negroes" and complained that Maria Juana had "corrupted" other slaves "by word of mouth and in writing" (Blake, n.d., Supp. Vol. V, p. 366). This last comment suggests that María Juana was literate and resourceful. In 1808, she petitioned the governor of Spanish Texas to allow her to buy the freedom of her 28-year-old son, Santiago (or "Jacques") who had escaped (Haggard, 1942). Although Bernardo sent his lawyer to protest, the sale was granted by the chief civil authority in San Antonio. D'Ortolan received 400 pesos for "the slave Santiago to remain free and in the possession of his mother María Juana" (p. 59). One hundred and sixty pesos were paid up front, and 240 pesos were due in five months.

Later in 1808, an even darker story involving D'Ortolan and an enslaved African creole emerged. Bernardo and his legitimate son, Raymond, were jailed for the latter's severe beating of an enslaved person named Lorenzo Maret (Haggard. 1942, p. 43, 58-59). The father was culpable because he witnessed the abuse and did not intervene. The Commandant of Nacogdoches, José Guadina, ordered an examination and protection of the slave pending his master's trial. His comments suggested that this would be very bad press for new slaves in the territory coming from Louisiana and such beatings were not acceptable in Nacogdoches territory. The lead Spanish Texas judicial official in San Antonio released the D'Ortolan pair for time served and returned Lorenzo to them with a strong warning against any future abuse. He further decreed, "should he [Lorenzo] find some person in these territories who wishes to buy him, his masters must agree to the sale" (p. 115). The commandant of the Nacogdoches post was advised to insure that Lorenzo was appropriately treated. Interestingly, Raymond, notwithstanding this abusive behavior toward an enslaved African creole man, later had a long common-law marriage with a free female of African descent from Natchitoches and fathered six mulatto children with her. She and her children were the D'Ortolan heirs after Raymond's death in 1838 (Blake, n.d., Vol. XXX, p. 231, 234).

Despite this suggestion of cruelty, Bernardo D'Ortolan left his land grant in 1813 under the care of María Juana's younger son, Raphael. Bernardo never returned to his rancho on the Loco Bayou in modern western Nacogdoches County but did set Raphael free in his Last Will and Testimony probated in 1820, "Item first, it is my wish that my negro man slave named Raphael aged thirty-five years who has been a true and faithful servant to me be emancipated from and after the day of my decease" (Natchitoches Parish Court House, Book 2, April 1816-March 1820, p. 459-462). His neighbor, Joseph de la Baume did the same, freeing his slave Narciso by 1809 and leaving him in charge of his large rancho on the Loco Creek (UTITCSA, 1975, Vol. 2, p. 240, 266).

Bernardo D'Ortolan's sojourn in Nacogdoches extended from 1796 until the summer of 1813 when he was forced to leave Texas because of his participation along with many other locals in the failed Magee-Guitterez revolt against Spain. Bernardo died outside Natchitoches, LA in 1820. His legitimate son, Raymond, inherited Rancho San Bernardo but generally remained in Natchitoches with his common-law wife, a free African-American woman named Marie Perot, and their six children. Raymond, his wife, children and six slaves are noted in the 1828 and 1829 census for Nacogdoches (UTITCSA, 1975). We also know that Raymond's son-in-law, Victor La Brun, returned to live on the land briefly in 1827 (Blake, n.d., Vol. XXX, p. 170). The D'Ortolan heirs lost control of the original grant to Anglo settlers in the 1840's.

The story of Bernardo D'Ortolan illustrates the subtle contrasts between treatment of African individuals during the Spanish Colonial period in East Texas and the later Anglo Texian/American period beginning in the 1830's. The Spanish officially made slavery illegal but tolerated the practice in Texas. There were a number of free "people of color" in Natchitoches and eastern Texas; intermarriage was not uncommon between persons of African descent and those of European and Native American lineage. As we have seen, slaves had the right to appeal to legal authority for protection and the right to gain their freedom. Once free, Africans were treated as "citizens." Even as enslaved persons, these early residents of East Texas were able to tend their own animals, raise their own crops, and engage in commerce on the side.

Raphael D'Ortolan

A Natchitoches parish record from October 9, 1788 stated: "baptism of Raphael, aged about one month, *negro*, father unknown, property of Mr. Dortolant" (UTITCSA, 1975, Vol. 2, p. 367, 383). Raphael D'Ortolan accompanied his master, Bernardo D'Ortolan, and his enslaved mother, Maria Juana, to Nacogdoches at eight years of age. He was a part of a community of enslaved persons numbering seven to twelve living on D'Ortolan's Rancho

Bernardo del Loco ten miles west of Nacogdoches. Little is known of Raphael's childhood except that his mother and older brother departed the Rancho apparently on bad terms when he was a teenager. Raphael was mature and responsible enough at age 25 to be left in charge of the D'Ortolan rancho when Bernardo had to flee the Nacogdoches district due to his involvement in the Magee-Gutierrez revolt in 1813. Raphael was emancipated in 1820 at the death of his master. The African creole was likely occupied with farming and ranching while maintaining the integrity of the rancho and occasionally playing host to visitors and travelers on the *El Camino Real* who stayed in the main house.

For the next 18 years, Raphael D'Ortolan lived as a free man on the land where he had resided since a boy. The Mexican censuses of 1833 and 1834 noted him to be a "laborer" (UTITCSA, 1975). Raphael was found on the 1837 Republic of Texas Tax List (Ericson, 1991). He married Josefa Lopes (born about 1802), and the couple had three children: Juan Jose (b. ~ 1825), Maria Polinaria (b. ~ 1827) and a child born in the early 1830's who did not survive infancy (UTITCSA, 1975). In 1837, Raphael executed a bond for $1000 with Marie Perot D'Ortolan, Bernardo's daughter-in-law and heir to the Rancho, and he agreed to pay her $25 per year for the right to continue to live on the land (Blake, n.d., Vol. XXI, p. 170).

As evidence of his free legal status, Raphael D'Ortolan gave testimony during December 1827 in a civil matter regarding a boundary line dispute between his neighbors, Joseph de la Baume and the heirs of Francisco de los Santos Coy (Blake, n.d., Vol. XII, p. 229-230). During his deposition he was referred to as "Citizen Rafael Dortolan." Although he was a person of modest means, Raphael was civically minded and supported community efforts. In 1829 he contributed the use of "one young ox for three days" as part of "the citizens of the Town of Nacogdoches who subscribe and contribute for the rebuilding of the Church" (Blake, n.d., Vol. XII, p. 95). Raphael gave $2.00 in 1830 and was listed with "individuals who voluntarily. . . offered assistance for the campaign against the enemy nations of Comanches, Taguacanos and Waco" (Blake, n.d., Vol. XVI, p. 269).

Raphael D'Ortolan's life underwent a radical change as Anglo Americans poured into eastern Texas in the late 1820s and early 1830s. When the Republic of Texas won its independence from Mexico in 1836, many members of longtime Hispanic families, African and mulatto freedmen, and Native Americans found themselves disenfranchised and dispossessed. Under the leadership of Nacogdoches native Vicente Cordova, a group of 100 multi-ethnic Mexican loyalists revolted against the new Anglo-dominated Republic in August 1838 (Blake, n.d., Vol. LIII, p. 311-326). Despite some skirmishes with Texians, the Cordova Rebellion group hid in the East Texas woods until March 1839. Then they attempted to escape by traveling overland to Matamoros, Mexico because promised aid from France and Mexico did not arrive. Raphael D'Ortolan was with this group, now diminished to less than sixty souls (Freeman, 2004; Nance, 1963; Sowell, 1991).

On March 28, 1839 near Mill Creek in the Guadalupe River valley five miles east of Seguin, Colonel Edward Burleson attacked the fleeing Cordova party killing almost half of the rebels. "Nineteen men were taken as prisoners, including three Negroes" (Freeman, 2004, p. 127). Cordova escaped to Mexico.

The Texian chroniclers described the captured and wounded Raphael as a "large French Negro" weighing around two hundred pounds (Nance, 1963, p. 127). His fellow African freedmen included an irascible, old gray-headed Black man who stated that he had once worked in the Capote Hills nearby (Freeman, 2004). Interestingly, the Capote Hills were owned by none other than Joseph de la Baume, who bought part of Bernardo D'Ortolan's Nacogdoches land grant 35 years before (Williams, 1997, p. 314). This man may have been Raphael's neighbor, Narciso de la Baume, who would have been about 70 years old at the time (Blake, n.d., Vol. LIII, p. 311-326). Another, less likely possible identity of this elderly man would have been Joshua N. Robertson, the only other male of color besides Raphael to be indicted as part of the Cordova rebellion (Blake, n.d.). The third Black person was a teenage boy who had been shot at least four times and stabbed repeatedly, yet survived.

The Anglos decided to sell the three Black captives to earn a little money for their trouble. The older two African creoles asserted that they had lived most of their adult lives as freedmen and would not go back into slavery. Raphael was quoted to have said, "Now, if you turn us loose we will go to Mexico and promise to never bother White folks again. We won't be a slave again, we have been free too long" (Freeman, 2004, p.27). Perhaps to intimidate his captors, the older Black man said he had once killed his White master's family (Freeman, 2004, p. 27). These factors led the Texian officers to court martial the two older captives and sentence them to death. The young boy agreed to be sold back into slavery. He was bought at auction for $451. Shortly after, the boy went swimming and was never seen again (Freeman, 2004, p. 29).

The morning after the court martial, Raphael D'Ortolan and the older Black man were marched out into the countryside a half-mile west of the Texian camp in Seguin. They were ordered to dig their own graves. The older man was stoic, but Raphael, perhaps thinking of his wife and children back in East Texas, begged for his life. His appeal was denied. Both men were forced to kneel down. They were blind folded, shot, and fell into their graves (Freeman, 2004, p. 28).

Thus, the 50 year long life of Raphael D'Ortolan ended. He spent more than 42 years living along Mill Branch, a tributary of Bayou Loco in western Nacogdoches County. He was born a slave in a French-speaking frontier town, lived on a Spanish Colonial rancho, and died as a freedman and rebel at the hands of the early Texian military far from home. Nothing is known of what became of his family or descendants. His life represents part of the untold story of African creoles in Texas.

In 1975, Dr. Jim Corbin of Stephen F. Austin State University discovered the stone outline of a house he believed to be the "slave quarters" of the Bernardo D'Ortolan rancho near Lake Nacogdoches (Story, 1982, p. 9, 51-53). Subsequent archeological investigations from 2003 to 2009 have identified a second building at the "Raphael Site" (AEC, 2008, 41NA300). Artifacts from this research have included European ceramics, machine cut nails, a pair of scissors (perhaps used by Josefa Lopes D'Ortolan) and a spur (perhaps that belonging to Raphael). In October 2009, a crew of local African Americans participated in an archeological excavation of one of the earliest-known African sites in Texas (Jackson, Middlebrook, Avery, Shafer, & Meissner, 2012, p. 241-245).

Conclusions

Much of the literature dealing with Black History in Texas focuses on the period of Anglo ascendancy after 1830. Previously, Africans had a variety of experiences during French and Spanish colonial rule. While most Black people were enslaved, there were a number of free "people of color" in East Texas. Intermarriage was not uncommon between people of African descent and persons of European and Native American lineage. African slaves had certain rights under Spanish rule that would not be enjoyed by slaves in the United States. They could appeal to the Spanish governor or courts for protection from inappropriate treatment by their masters and for the redress of grievances. Slaves were given some opportunity to plant their own crops and sell their products in the market (Blake, n.d., Vol. V, p. 352-376). Some slaves were allowed to buy their own freedom. Much of this would change with the coming of the Republic of Texas.

While we know little of the fine-grained details of Raphael D'Ortolan's life, the larger themes of his biography and character are clear. First, he was born into slavery and died a freedman. Unlike his mother and brother, Raphael's path to freedom was through loyalty to his master and faithful responsibility. He bought his freedom not with pesos but with service. Was he tempted to run off from Rancho Bernardo del Loco when he was clearly out of the reach of his master en absentia after 1813? This remains a mystery, but he stayed at his post for eight years after his owner left for Louisiana and died there. Second, when Raphael gained his freedom, he joined the community as a responsible citizen. He worked, married, fathered children, participated in community fundraising, loaned out his property to help the Church, gave testimony in Court, signed a bond, paid rent, and paid taxes. In all these ways, Raphael was a typical citizen in the Nacogdoches free community. From 1821 until 1838, he was a Black man, a free man, and a member of society. Third, when the time came, Raphael demonstrated conviction and courage. He was understandably outraged by the usurpation of land and power by newcomers who threatened the century-old Hispanic world that existed in Nacogdoches and that he had lived in for over four decades. Raphael joined his neighbors and many community leaders in a vain attempt to throw off the interlopers and their selectively repressive regime, as the rebels saw it. He took a courageous stand with the very people who had accepted him into a free society. But the Texian tide was too high, and it swallowed up the Cordova Rebellion. When he was tracked down, wounded and captured, his courage was tested again. He was given the choice of slavery and life, or freedom and certain death. From the standpoint of Anglo-centric values of his times, Raphael D'Ortolan was a traitor and was executed following a court-martial. From a 21st Century perspective, he was a genuine hero of Texas history. He embraced freedom, refused to let it go, and died as a free citizen of Texas rather than be a slave to any man.

Acknowledgments

I am deeply indebted to Susan Holley of Bastrop, Louisiana who has provided much information based on her extensive research of Bernardo D'Ortolan. As a direct lineal descendent of Bernardo D'Ortolan, she is his most important biographer. Ms. Holley has shared research leads and many copies of documents that she has unearthed. Her continued support and friendship is greatly appreciated.

References

Archeological & Environmental Consultants (AEC) (2008). *Archeological investigations at the D'Ortolan Site (41NA299) and other late 18th century to early 20th century sites along bayou loco in western Nacogdoches county, Texas*. (No. 63). Austin, TX: Perttula, T. K. Archives Municipales de Bordeaux. (n.d.).Sacramental Registers of Ste-Croix, [CG 256, act 1387).

Blake, R. B. (n.d.) Research Collection and Supplement. Ninety-three volumes of transcriptions and translations of materials pertaining to the history of East Texas and Nacogdoches County. East Texas Collection, Stephen F. Austin State University, Nacogdoches.

Burton, H. S., & Smith, F. T. (2008) *Colonial Natchitoches: A Creole community on the Louisiana-Texas frontier*. College Station, TX: Texas A&M University Press.

Byrd, K. M. (2008) *Colonial Natchitoches: Outpost of empires*. Xlibris: Place Chipman, D. E.(2010). Estevanico. *Handbook of Texas Online*. Published by the Texas State Historical Association. Retrieved from http://www.tshaonline.org/handbook/online/articles/fes08 Ericson, C. R. (1991). Nacogdoches – gateway to Texas: A biographical directory 1773 – 1849. 1. Nacogdoches, TX: Ericson Books.

Chipman, D. E. (2010). Estevanico. *Handbook of Texas Online*. Published by the Texas State Historical Association. Retrieved from http://www.tshaonline.org/handbook/online/articles/fes08

Ericson, C. R. (1991). *Nacogdoches – gateway to Texas: A biographical directory* 1773 – 1849. 1. Nacogdoches, TX: Ericson Books.

Freeman, L. (2004). *The Cordova rebellion: An examination of the reaction to American intrusion in the Louisiana – Texas borderland*, 1812-1842 (Unpublished master's thesis). Northwestern State University of Louisiana, Natchitoches, LA.

Haggard, J. V. (1942). *Translation of Spanish archives*. University of Texas, Austin.

Hatcher, M. A. (1926). A Texas border ballad. In F. Dobie (Ed.), *Rainbow in the morning, Publication of the Texas Folklore Society*, 5, Southern Methodist University, Dallas, TX.

Jackson, M. K., Middlebrook, T., Avery, G., Shafer, H., & Meissner, B. (2012). *Trade and cultural Interaction along El Camino Real de los Tejas during the Spanish colonial and republic periods in Nacogdoches county, Texas*. 2 Vols. Nine Flags Museum, Nacogdoches, TX.

Mills, E. S. (1977). *Natchitoches, abstracts of the Catholic church registers of the French and Spanish post of St. Jean Baptiste des Natchitoches in Louisiana*: 1729-1803. New Orleans, LA: Polyanthos.

Mills, E. S. (1980). *Natchitoches, translated abstracts of register number five of the Catholic church parish of St. Francois des Natchitoches in Louisiana*: 1800-1826. Westminster: Heritage Books.

Nance, J. M. (1963). *The Cordova-Flores incident after San Jacinto: The Texas-Mexican Frontier*, 1836-1841. Austin, TX: University of Texas Press.

Natchitoches Parish Court House. (April 1816- March 1820). Book 2, 459-462.

Ocaruz, J. J. A. (1964). The Natchitoches revolt. *Louisiana Studies*, 3(1), 117-132.

Residents of Texas, 1782-1836, Volumes 1, 2, 3. (1984). Nacogdoches, TX: Ericson Books.

Sowell, A. J.(1991). *Rangers and pioneers of Texas*. Austin, TX: State House Press.

Story, D. A. (1982). *The Deshazo site, Nacogdoches County, Volume 1*. Texas Antiquities Committee, Austin, TX.

The University of Texas Institute of Texas Cultures at San Antonio (UTITCSA) (1975). *Texas and the American revolution*. The University of Texas at San Antonio, Institute of Texas Cultures, San Antonio.

The University of Texas Institute of Texas Cultures at San Antonio (UTITCSA) (1984). *Texas and the American Revolution*. The University of Texas at San Antonio, Institute of Texas Cultures, San Antonio.

Walker, J. P. (1806). Map from Nacogdoches to San Pedro Mission. Initialed "J.P.W." Berlandier Papers, New Haven, CT: Yale University.

Williams, E. R. (1997). *Encyclopedia of individuals and founding families of the Ouachita valley of Louisiana from 1785 to 1850, Part Two, L-O*.

East Texas: From Post Civil Rights to the Obama Era

By: Dr. Dianne Dentice

Introduction and Historical Backdrop

East Texas is considered by geographers to be the westernmost extension of the Deep South. The predominant cultural influence comes from customs and traditions passed down from Anglo and African southerners along with Mexican immigrants who settled the region during the mid-to-late nineteenth century. To this day, most residents of East Texas tend to be predominantly non-Catholic Christians who express their faith in denominations that include Baptist (particularly Southern Baptist), Methodist, Presbyterian, Lutheran, and Pentecostal. Catholicism is also an influence due to the fact that Mexican-origin immigrants eventually became citizens and retained their religion.

Some East Texans identify specifically with cowboy culture. Others are likely to align themselves with small farming traditions indigenous to this part of the state. Additionally, it is common for many East Texans to own and trade cattle. There are several "sale barns" across the region that host weekly and monthly trade events, as is common in parts of the lower Southern region of the United States. Because of the location, geography, and culture of East Texas, its ties with the South are more pronounced than other regions of the state. Texas also joined the Confederacy during the Civil War and its southern connections became historical fact.

Nacogdoches County is in the middle of what is also referred to as the Piney Woods region of East Texas. The county seat, Nacogdoches, bills itself as the oldest town in Texas. In 1800 Nacogdoches was the second-largest settlement in Texas with a population of 297 residents plus 103 slaves (Faulk, 1964). By 1840 the county reported 197 slave owners the largest being John M. Durst with thirty-nine slaves. In addition to its Spanish-speaking population, the town was home to a contingent of French speaking traders who migrated from Louisiana. Because of its location, Nacogdoches became a leading entry way for Anglo immigrants, earning the title "Gateway to Texas" (Long, 2010). As a further sign of the city's growth and progress, Stephen F. Austin State University was founded in 1923 as a teacher's college and is one of four independent public institutions of higher learning in the state.

The Civil Rights Era

During the 1960s, both African Americans and Mexican Americans took part in national movements to bring down racial barriers. Black Texans held demonstrations throughout the state to protest segregation. They also instituted boycotts of racist merchants. In conjunction with the National March on Washington in 1963, approximately 900 protesters marched in Austin. The protestors included a coalition of Latino, Hispanic, Black, and White citizens attacking Governor John Connally's failure to support the pending civil-rights bill in Washington, D.C. (De León & Calvert, 2010). By the late 1960s, some segments of the Black community joined the Black power movement in opposition to Martin Luther King's more benign civil rights initiative. By the 1970s, the Black Panthers had been virtually wiped out by law enforcement authorities, Malcolm X was dead, and integration was occurring throughout the South, including Texas.

Much of the activity in civil rights during the last quarter of the twentieth century and the opening decade of the new millennium focused on consolidating the gains of previous decades. For example, African Americans registered to vote in unprecedented numbers, and Black candidates eventually won election to major local, state, and federal offices. Issues such as affirmative action in higher education remained, but the civil rights movement permanently changed the social and political landscape of Texas. In Nacogdoches, integration was not a smooth process and did not begin until the early 1970s (Delear, 2011).

On May 13, 1970, civil rights marchers were met by local police west of Church Street. This event marked the culmination of many years of racial conflict and resulted in two days of rioting. The forces that compelled White town residents to take up arms and confront civil rights demonstrators began back in 1929 when African American residents were forced to move into the Orton Hill neighborhood, east of downtown. A ploy by Whites to secure valuable property and displace Black business owners appears to have been the motive (Delear, 2011). Needless to say, relations between the races became strained and continued to be so for years to come.

Sundown Towns and White Supremacy

A sundown town is a town where certain groups of people are allowed to work during the day but must be out of town and into their own communities by the time the sun goes down (Loewen, 2005). In the South, the group primarily affected by this unwritten law was African Americans. Texas is believed to have had several of these towns that include Grand Saline and Vidor, both located in the East Texas region. Although Nacogdoches has not been officially documented a sundown town, in view of its troublesome past with the African American community, a critical reading of historical documents may indicate otherwise.

Just as sundown towns were an extreme form of exclusion and discrimination, the Ku Klux Klan was an organized presence in the South (and other regions of the country) beginning in the Reconstruction era. In fact, many sundown towns depended on the Klan to enforce curfews and punish Blacks who did not comply (MacLean, 1994; Wade, 1987). During the civil-rights era of the late 1950s and early 1960s, Klan activity in Texas increased somewhat, but because of new anti-Klan laws and FBI pressure, the organization remained small and politically irrelevant. Subsequently, the Klan fractured into numerous small cells (Long, 2010). During the early 1980s the Klan gained notoriety for its attacks on Vietnamese shrimpers along the Gulf Coast and in the early 1990s it was again in the news because of assaults on Black residents in Vidor who were trying to move into an all white apartment complex.

Affirmative action, deindustrialization, and the increase in multiculturalism are seen as attacks on White identity and White culture by segments of the White population, some of whom join extremist groups. The South with its distinct regional identity has spawned neo-Confederate groups such as League of the South whose primary goal is to restore southern culture (Hague & Sebesta, 2008). This appeal to both ethnicity and nationality is an attempt to define White identity as part of the larger stage of identity politics in the United States. It also allows racist discourse to flourish in mainstream society by providing an avenue for discussion of White identity within the context of southern pride without the burden of Nazi symbols and burning crosses. With a secessionist streak embedded in Texas culture and history, White supremacy takes many forms.

A Regional Snapshot

Analyzing racial attitudes has long been a focus for social scientists, and findings continue to change as American society becomes more diverse. Link and Oldendick (1996) found that mainstream White Americans tend to view racial minorities less positively than they do their own race. During the time of their study they concluded that the social distance between White respondents and Asian Americans was smaller than for African Americans. Attitudes toward Hispanics fell somewhere in-between the two extremes. Quillian's (1996) findings indicate that traditional prejudice has declined in every U.S. region except the South. He also concluded that racial attitudes in the South were more hostile toward Blacks because of group threat based on population patterns within that region, particularly in urban areas. Even more telling was Gallagher's (2003) finding that "the average American" perceives the population of blacks to be twice the actual number (p. 381). He concluded that the media, residential segregation, and racial stereotypes all contribute to underestimation of the size of the White population (among Whites) and inflation of group size of racial minorities (especially Blacks) which results in unsubstantiated perceptions of group threat. With those findings in mind, I will discuss the following East Texas towns from a not yet post-racial perspective: Nacogdoches, Big Sandy, and Jasper.

Nacogdoches

The population of Nacogdoches is documented at 32,642 (98% urban and 2% rural). Roughly 49% of the population is White and 31% is African American (City of Nacogdoches Data, 2013). Approximately 54.6% of the White population in Nacogdoches would have to move to other neighborhoods in order to achieve full integration (CensusScope Dissimilarity Index, 2014). About 20.9% of Nacogdoches families (all races) are documented as living below the poverty line, including 38.4% of children under the age of 18. A total of 50% of the African American population is documented as living in poverty compared to 26% of Whites. Income inequality does not necessarily mean that race relations will be strained. However, when groups are segregated, the class divide adds another level of stress (Feagin & Feagin, 2012). Additionally, by the 1970s when integration occurred, the statute of limitations had run on reclamation of real estate taken in 1929 when Black business owners were driven out of the downtown area, and Black residents were forced into the Orton Hill neighborhoods. Long time African American residents of Nacogdoches lost their ability to regain stolen property, and the current poverty statistics reveal their fate.

To add insult to injury, White city leaders systematically erased the memory of the civil rights era in Nacogdoches. In the early 1990s, contractors were hired by the city to prepare a National Register application for the Zion Hill Historic District, spared by the displacement of Black citizens to Orton Hill in 1929. The report inaccurately noted that there were no documented efforts by White citizens to move Blacks to "camps" outside of town. The Orton Hill area, the "camp" where African Americans were moved, did not receive a national register nomination. For these reasons, among others, the African American community of Nacogdoches has lost its history of struggle and violence to the dustbin of revisionist White history. In 1999, the city closed the Arthur Temple Swimming Pool in the Orton Hill area; which served as a social chub for the African American community since the 1950s. Many people viewed the pool's closing as another attack on African American communal history and identity.

Big Sandy

Big Sandy is a small East Texas community located at the junction of State Highway 155, U.S. Highway 80, and Farm Road 2911 in Upshur County. The most recent town census indicates that the total population of the town is 1343, and it is listed as 100 rural (City of Big Sandy Data, 2013). Whites make up 82% of the population followed by 13% African American and 5% Hispanic. Approximately 21% of people living in Big Sandy are below the poverty line. Of the White population, 14% live in poverty compared to 42% of the African American population. Mapping of the community also indicates extreme segregation between the Black and White communities, even though the public housing projects were successfully integrated during the 1990s.

In March 2012, a White man walked into the Two Rivers Grocery and Market in Big Sandy. He shopped for groceries and when he went to check out and pay for his food, a young African American employee began bagging his groceries. According to a journalist, Sarah Thomas (2012), because of his religious beliefs the shopper stated that a Black man could not touch his food. The cashier asked a White employee to finish bagging the man's groceries.

He paid and left. Later the owner of the store, Keith Langston who is White, found out about the incident. He told his employees that this customer would not be allowed to shop there in the future. Two days later the customer reappeared, and Langston called authorities to remove him from the premises. In the newspaper article, the customer is quoted as stating that his civil and religious rights were violated with the ban and that under the law, White people have the same protections as "Negroids." Subsequently the customer filed a lawsuit against the owner of the grocery store that was thrown out by the judge.

Jasper

One of the more notorious East Texas towns is Jasper, located about 130 miles northeast of Houston and 82 miles south of Nacogdoches. In July 2013 the population was recorded at 7,656 with a demographic breakdown of 49% White and 45% African American (City of Jasper Data, 2013). Approximately 28% of the White population lives in poverty when compared to 40% of the African American population. Some other significant city statistics include that the median household income is below Texas state average, the African American population is significantly above state average, and the Hispanic population percentage is significantly below state average.

Jasper achieved national prominence in 1998 when three White men with ties to the Aryan Brotherhood prison gang, murdered a Black man named James Byrd, Jr. by dragging him to death behind a pickup truck. Subsequently all three men were found guilty, two of them were sentenced to death, and the other received a life sentence. In June 2012, after 16 months in office, Jasper's first African American police chief, Rodney Pearson, was fired by the newly elected city council. New council members argued that he was not qualified for the job even though he had 22 years of experience as a state trooper and had served as the town's volunteer fire chief in 2009. An all-White group called the League of Concerned Citizens also petitioned to recall four Black council members who had voted to hire Mr. Pearson. According to a lawsuit filed in connection with the recall effort, not a single African American citizen signed the petition (Fernandez, 2012). When the new council was elected in May 2012, it became a 4-to-1 White majority. As of June 2014, it is still a 4-to-1 White majority, and the elected county commissioners are five White males.

Closing Remarks

Racism in its most manifest form is revealed in cross burnings, lynchings, and swastikas scrawled across synagogue walls. After a bitter few years of integration efforts in Nacogdoches, African American civil rights leaders began to try to get representation on the city council. As cited by Delear (2011) organizers had to fight editorial propaganda from the *Daily Sentinel*: "we cannot afford to let minority groups elect candidates in local elections" (p. 144). Eventually, voting rights suits created more equitable county districts, which resulted in the election of Amos Henderson, an African-American preacher, to County Commissioner. He became the first African-American County Commissioner elected in East Texas in the twentieth century and the first African American elected to public office in Nacogdoches since Reconstruction. Today, the county commissioner's court is represented by four White men and the city council is a 4-to-1 White majority. Mr. Roy Boldon who represents the Southeast Ward, is the only African American council member.

The East Texas region has made some progress as evidenced by the overwhelming response by co-workers and owner of the small grocery in Big Sandy when an employee was verbally harassed by a racist customer. Unfortunately, for every step forward, some communities take two steps back. When Mr. Pearson, the African American police chief in Jasper was recalled, numerous racial epithets appeared on Facebook pages and other social media. The cemetery where Mr. Byrd is buried remains segregated and African Americans are underrepresented in both city and county government.

Race is not just an issue for Texas and specifically the East Texas region. President Obama has endured his own share of racial innuendos during his two terms in office. In 2008, former Democratic vice-presidential candidate, Geraldine Ferraro, had no problem claiming that Barack Obama had ascended solely because of the color of his skin. When reporters challenged her reasoning, she shot back with the following statement: "You are only attacking me because I'm White" (Ridley, 2008). It is ironic that the late Ms. Ferraro who was of Italian heritage conveniently forgot that at one time in our nation's history her ethnic group was labeled a distinct race and perceived by the dominant group as undesirable immigrants. Until we, as a society, can come to grips with our own biases – no matter what our political persuasion - bigotry will continue to raise its ugly head and progress toward racial and ethnic tolerance will sputter and stall.

References

CensusScope. (2014). *Segregation dissimilarity indices Nacogdoches, Texas* [Data file]. Retrieved from http://www.censusscope.org/segregation.html

City of Big Sandy. (2013). [Data file]. Retrieved from http://www.city-data.com/city/Big-Sandy-Texas html#ixzz34Gy0WyEH

City of Jasper. (2013). [Data file]. Retrieved from http://www.city-data.com/city/Jasper-Texas.html#ixzz34SlyHJQf

City of Nacogdoches. (2013). [Data file]. Retrieved from http://www.city-data.com/city/Nacogdoches-Texas html#ixzz320w57byo

Delear, S. (2011). *March! The fight for civil rights in a land of fear: Nacogdoches, Texas 1929-1975*. (Unpublished master's thesis). Stephen F. Austin State University, Nacogdoches, Texas.

De León, A., & Calvert, R. A. (2010) Civil Rights. *Handbook of Texas online.* Retrieved from http://www.tshaonline.org/handbook/online/articles/pkcfl

Faulk, O. B. (1964). The Penetration of foreigners and foreign i into Spanish east Texas, 1793–1810. *East Texas Historical Journal*, 2, 87-98.

Feagin, J. R., & Feagin, C. B. (2008). *Racial and ethnic relations*. Upper Saddle River, NJ: Pearson.

Fernandez, M. (2012, June 21). Racial tensions flare anew in a Texas town. *The New York Times*. Retrieved from http://www.nytimes.com/2012/06/22/us/in-jasper-texas-racial-tensions-flare-again.html?_r=0

Gallagher, C. (2003). Miscounting ace: Explaining Whites' misconceptions of racial group size. *Sociological Perspectives*, 46, 381-396.

Hague, E., & Sebesta, E. H. (2008). Neo-confederacy, culture, and ethnicity: A White anglo-Celtic southern people. In E. Hague, H. Beirich, & E. H. Sebesta (Eds.), *Neo-Confederacy*. Austin, Texas: University of Texas Press.

Handbook of Texas Online. (2010). Ku Klux Klan. Retrieved from http://www.tshaonline.org/handbook/online/articles/vek02

Link, M. W., & Oldendick, R. W. (1996). Social construction and White attitudes toward equal opportunity and multiculturalism. *The Journal of Politics*, 58, 149-168.

Loewen, J. (2005). *Sundown towns*. New York, NY: Touchstone.

Long, C. (2010). Nacogdoches County. *Handbook of Texas Online*. Retrieved from http://www.tshaonline.org/handbook/online/articles/hcn01

MacLean, N. (1994). *Behind the mask of chivalry: The making of the second Ku Klux Klan*. New York, NY: Oxford University Press.

Quillian, L. (1996). Group threat and regional change in attitudes toward African Americans. *American Journal of Sociology*, 102, 816-860.

Ridley, J. (2008). Why we hate. Retrieved from http://www.esquire.com/print-this/hatred-0608

Thomas, S. (2012, August 8). Lawsuit claims Black sacker, ban from Big Sandy grocery store violated customer's rights. *Longview News-Journal*. Retrievied from http://www.news-journal.com/news/2012/aug/08/lawsuit-claims-black-sacker-ban-from-big-sandy-gro/

Wade, W. C. (1987). *The fiery cross: The Ku Klux Klan in America*. New York, NY: Simon and Schuster.

The Changing Racial and Hispanic Composition of Nacogdoches and Its Educational Institutions

By: Dr. Robert F. Szafran

The Nacogdoches Independent School District (NISD) formally integrated its schools in 1970. In the years since then, the racial and Hispanic composition of the students enrolled in NISD has changed substantially as has the composition of the school-age populations of the City of Nacogdoches and the county in which it is located, Nacogdoches County. This chapter will document those changes along with racial and Hispanic shifts in the general populations of the city, county, and State of Texas. It will also report on changes in the composition of Stephen F. Austin State University's (SFASU) student enrollment and the corresponding changes in the college-age population in the regions of Texas from which SFASU draws most of its students. These race and Hispanic demographic profiles can provide a context to better understand the actions of the city and its institutions as well as the experiences of its citizens.

All of the data for this chapter come from official sources—the U.S. Decennial Census of Population, the Texas Educational Association (TEA), and SFASU. The decennial census years (1970, 1980, 1990, 2000, and 2010) are used to document shifts in the racial and Hispanic composition of populations and student bodies. One exception to those time points is NISD enrollment in 1970. Because neither TEA nor NISD could provide 1970 racial and Hispanic enrollment numbers for the district, NISD enrollment figures for the closest available year, 1968, were used as estimates for the 1970 numbers (see Appendix).

Acknowledgements for assistance: Kayce Halstead, Amber Middleton, Larissa Philpot, Charles Ashton, and Jere Jackson.

Correspondence concerning this chapter should be addressed to Robert F. Szafran, Department of Anthropology, Geography and Sociology, Stephen F. Austin State University, Box 13047 SFA Station, Nacogdoches, Texas. rszafran@sfasu.edu.

Measuring Race, Hispanic Origin, and Place of Residence

It is important to recognize at the outset that the measurement of race and Hispanic status is difficult and, inevitably, somewhat arbitrary. As the U.S. Bureau of the Census has regularly stated (1973, 1982, 1992, 2002, 2012a), its classification of race (and Hispanic status) does not reflect a scientific analysis or taxonomy. In the years covered in this chapter, the Census Bureau determined race and Hispanic status largely on the basis of individual self-reports. And that self-reporting is itself affected by the directions and categories presented to the individual by the Census Bureau. Those directions and categories have changed since 1970 as Figure 1 describes.

Every U.S. Census has classified individuals by race. Prior to 1970, racial classification was done largely by census takers' judgments. Starting with the 1970 Census, racial classification became a matter of self-report. For that self-report, individuals were presented with a list of race categories and also provided an option to specify a race not listed. Only starting with the 2000 Census could an individual self-report more than one race. Thus far, only a small percentage of individuals have chosen to report multiple-race identity on the census: 2.4% in 2000, 2.9% in 2010.

The 1970 Census was also the first to attempt an accurate estimate of the Hispanic population not just at the national level but at state, county, and city levels as well. That year 5% of all census forms directly inquired about Hispanic origin for each individual in the household; 15% of all census forms asked about language primarily spoken within the household; and that same 15% of returns were checked for probable Hispanic origin based on surname. These sample results were then extrapolated to entire populations. Starting with the 1980 census, Hispanic origin was asked on all census forms.

Because the Census Bureau assumes most people consider Hispanic status to be an ethnic or cultural characteristic and not a racial or physical characteristic, the Census Bureau separates the identification of race from the identification of Hispanic status. In practice, this has been difficult. When asked their race, most Hispanics respond White, but a substantial minority indicates Mexican, Puerto-Rican, Spanish, or simply Hispanic (Gibson & Jung, 2002). These persons were recorded as White by the Census Bureau in the 1970 Census. Starting with the 1980 Census, however, the Census Bureau stopped reclassifying all Hispanics as racially White. Since 1980, persons reporting their race as Hispanic are included along with other less often reported racial groups in the residual category "other races." Efforts by the Census Bureau to separate Hispanic status and race continued. The 2000 Census moved the Hispanic question in front of the race question, and the 2010 Census included in the question about Hispanic status the statement "For this census, Hispanic origins are not races."

Confusion sometimes occurs regarding where persons attending college are counted by the U.S. Census. This matters for the present analysis because SFASU is located in the City of Nacogdoches and from 1970 through 2010 usually had an enrollment of 10,000 or more students. The Census Bureau has consistently stated that persons enrolled in school at the time of the census (April 1) should be counted where they normally reside while attending school. That means university students living in residence halls on campus or in apartments or homes off campus but within the city are included in the city's census totals even though those students might think of their home as where their family lives, where they are registered to vote, or some other place. University students commuting to classes from residences outside the

Figure 1
Measurement of Race and Hispanic Origin: 1970 Census and Subsequent Major Changes

1970 Census[a]
- Race
    - Self-reported
    - Directly asked on all census forms
    - Only one race category could be selected
    - Persons specifying Hispanic origin as their race were reclassified as white
    - Race question occurs before Hispanic Origin question
- Hispanic Origin
    - Self-reported
    - Directly asked on 5% sample of census forms; indirectly coded based on surname and primary language spoken in home on 15% sample of census forms

1980 Census Changes[b]
- Race
    - Persons specifying Hispanic origin as their race were included in residual "other races" category
- Hispanic Origin
    - Directly asked on all census forms

1990 Census Changes[c]
- Race
    - Only minor changes
- Hispanic Origin
    - Only minor changes

2000 Census Changes[d]
- Race

2010 Census Changes[e]
- Race
    - Only minor changes
- Hispanic Origin
    - Directions note that Hispanic origin is not considered a race

a U.S. Census Bureau (1973, Appendix B)
b U.S. Census Bureau (1982, Appendices B and E)
c U.S. Census Bureau (1992, Appendices B and E)
d U.S. Census Bureau (2002, Appendices B and D)
e U.S. Census Bureau (2012a, Appendices B and D)

city are not counted in city census totals but would be included in county totals unless they are commuting from outside the county.

A common concern regarding census figures is the number of persons missed by the census. Less publicized but also a problem are persons counted on more than one census form, for example, college students living away from home, persons serving in the military, and persons incarcerated. Recognizing this concern, the Bureau of the Census expends considerable effort in obtaining an accurate count. It estimated for the 2010 Census that Hispanics were undercounted by 1.5%, non-Hispanic Whites were overcounted by 0.8%, and non-Hispanic Blacks were undercounted by 2.1% (U.S. Census Bureau, 2012c).

How important are these methodological issues for understanding shifts in the racial and Hispanic composition of Nacogdoches and its educational institutions? They are probably of minor but not insignificant impact. Counts and percentage breakdowns of population groups reported in this chapter should be viewed as quite close but certainly not exact.

For reporting race and Hispanic status in this chapter a simple four-category breakdown will be used: non-Hispanic Whites, non-Hispanic Blacks, non-Hispanics who are neither White nor Black ("other races"), and Hispanics. Both U.S. Census and TEA publications frequently use this same four-category breakdown as do NISD and SFASU. To streamline the text from this point on, it should be understood that references to Whites, Blacks, and other races are, in fact, references to non-Hispanic Whites, non-Hispanic Blacks, and non-Hispanic other races. The specification "non-Hispanic" will be retained in tables, however.

General Population of Nacogdoches City, Nacogdoches County, and Texas

Table 1 tracks the changes in the total population of Nacogdoches City, Nacogdoches County, and the State of Texas from 1970 through 2010. The city population increased by 46% over this 40-year period—adding slightly more than 10,000 residents. It grew as a result of natural increase (births outnumbered deaths), net migration (in-migrants outnumbered out-migrants), and municipal annexation. However, while the city's growth was substantial, it failed to keep pace with the county which grew by 77% or with the state which grew by 125%.

The composition of the city's population became more diverse during this 40-year period with Hispanics and other races increasing their shares of the city population, Whites decreasing their share, and Blacks essentially maintaining their share.

The Hispanic share of the population increased from under 500 in 1970 to slightly over 5,500 in 2010—more than a ten-fold increase. Their share of the population increased from 2.1% to 16.8%. The Hispanic growth in the county paralleled the growth in the city, increasing from 2.7% to 17.6%. Although Hispanics have increased their share of both the city and the county population, they remain underrepresented in comparison to the state where Hispanics constituted 18.4% of the state population in 1970 and 37.6% in 2010.

Members of other races also increased their share of the city's population during this

Table 1

City, County, and State Populations for 1970 to 2010 (All Ages)

	Number of Persons					Percent of Population				
	1970[a]	1980[b]	1990[c]	2000[d]	2010[e]	1970	1980	1990	2000	2010
Nacogdoches City										
White (Non-Hispanic)	16,540	20,080	22,094	18,524	16,885	73.4%	74.0%	71.6%	61.9%	51.2%
Black (Non-Hispanic)	5,444	6,043	6,883	7,442	9,371	24.1%	22.3%	22.3%	24.9%	28.4%
Other Race (Non-Hispanic)	89	240	333	712	1,203	0.4%	0.9%	1.1%	2.4%	3.6%
Hispanic	471	786	1,562	3,236	5,537	2.1%	2.9%	5.1%	10.8%	16.8%
TOTAL	22,544	27,149	30,872	29,914	32,996	100.0%	100.1%	100.1%	100.0%	100.0%
Nacogdoches County										
White (Non-Hispanic)	27,664	37,218	42,575	41,620	39,699	76.1%	79.5%	77.8%	70.3%	61.5%
Black (Non-Hispanic)	7,606	7,920	8,948	9,815	11,573	20.9%	16.9%	16.3%	16.6%	17.9%
Other Race (Non-Hispanic)	122	328	442	1,108	1,896	0.3%	0.7%	0.8%	1.9%	2.9%
Hispanic	970	1,320	2,788	6,660	11,356	2.7%	2.8%	5.1%	11.2%	17.6%
TOTAL	36,362	46,786	54,753	59,203	64,524	100.0%	99.9%	100.0%	100.0%	99.9%
Texas										
White (Non-Hispanic)	7,657,457	9,350,297	10,291,680	10,933,313	11,397,345	68.4%	65.7%	60.6%	52.4%	45.3%
Black (Non-Hispanic)	1,399,005	1,692,542	1,976,360	2,364,255	2,886,825	12.5%	11.9%	11.6%	11.3%	11.5%
Other Race (Non-Hispanic)	80,597	200,528	378,565	884,586	1,400,470	0.7%	1.4%	2.2%	4.2%	5.6%
Hispanic	2,059,671	2,985,824	4,339,905	6,669,666	9,460,921	18.4%	21.0%	25.5%	32.0%	37.6%
TOTAL	11,196,730	14,229,191	16,986,510	20,851,820	25,145,561	100.0%	100.0%	99.9%	99.9%	100.0%

Note: Percentages may not total 100.0% due to rounding error. See Appendix for technical information on estimating numbers of Hispanics and non-Hispanic Whites, Blacks, and others.

[a] U.S. Census Bureau (1973, Tables 17, 27, 34, 60, 112, 129)
[b] U.S. Census Bureau (1982, Table 16)
[c] U.S. Census Bureau (1992, Tables 3, 5, 6)
[d] U.S. Census Bureau (2002, Table 3)
[e] U.S. Census Bureau (2012b, Table 3)

period from 0.4% to 3.6%. Of the 1,203 members of other races in the city in 2010, the largest groups were Native American, Filipino, and Chinese. Persons of other races made up a slightly larger share of the city's population than the county's population but a smaller share than the state's population.

Although the City of Nacogdoches' total population grew by over 10,000 persons from 1970 to 2010, there were just 345 more Whites living in the city in 2010 than in 1970. The number of Whites residing in the city grew by about 5,500 from 1970 through 1990 but then declined by almost that same amount by 2010. The White share of the population began this 40-year period at almost 75% of the population and ended the period at slightly above 50%.

Whites made up a greater share of the county's population than of the city's population but experienced a similar decline in both numbers and percent starting midway through the period. In the state, Whites declined from 68.4% on the population in 1970 to 45.3% in 2010; however, the actual number of Whites in Texas increased in each decade albeit by smaller and smaller amounts.

The city's Black population showed modest growth in numbers from 1970 through 2000, and, due to increased Black enrollment at SFASU, more substantial growth in the 2000s. Despite this growth in numbers, however, the Black share of the city's population increased only slightly during the period—24.1% in 1970 and 28.4% in 2010. In the county, Blacks increased in number each decade but, failing to keep pace with the growing number of Hispanics, ended the period in 2010 a smaller percent of the population (17.9%) than they began in 1970 (20.9%). Similar to the county, Blacks in the state increased in number each decade but declined slightly as a share of the population during the period.

NISD Enrollment and the 5 to 17 Year-Old Population

While NISD enrollment of Blacks and other races grew from 1970 through 2010, it was the changes in Hispanic and White enrollments that dramatically transformed the district. In 1970, as Table 2 shows, Hispanic students made up less than 1% of the district's enrollment and White students made up more than 60%. But in the 1980s Hispanic enrollment began to increase markedly and in the 1990s White enrollment began to decline. By 2010 Hispanic students made up 43.0% of the district's enrollment and were easily the largest racial/ethnic category of students while White students accounted for just 25.3% of the district's enrollment and trailed behind both Hispanics and Blacks in numbers. And the decline in White students was not just in percentages. In 2010 there was less than half the number of White students enrolled in the district as there was in 1990. These changes took place with no substantial alterations in the district's geographic boundaries between 1970 and 2010.

Changes in the racial and Hispanic composition of NISD from 1970 through 2010 can be compared to changes in the racial and Hispanic composition of the 5 through 17-year old population of the city and county (Table 2). Such comparisons should be made cautiously, however, for at least three reasons: First, while school districts draw almost all their enrollment from the 5 through 17 year-old population living in the district, recently added pre-kindergarten programs for children from low-income families typically enroll 4 year-olds. Second, persons missed in the decennial census count may still enroll in school. And third,

Table 2

NISD Enrollment and City and County 5 to 17 year-old Populations for 1970 to 2010

	Number of Persons					Percent of Enrollment or Population				
	1970	1980	1990	2000	2010	1970	1980	1990	2000	2010
NISD Enrollment[a]										
White (Non-Hispanic)	2,981[a]	3,040	3,527	2,668	1,633	63.7%	63.3%	59.4%	43.4%	25.3%
Black (Non-Hispanic)	1,665[a]	1,698	1,841	1,948	1,930	35.6%	35.4%	31.0%	31.7%	29.9%
Other Race (Non-Hispanic)	14[a]	17	41	58	124	0.3%	0.4%	0.7%	0.9%	1.9%
Hispanic	23[a]	44	526	1,478	2,777	0.5%	0.9%	8.9%	24.0%	43.0%
TOTAL	4,683[a]	4,799	5,935	6,152	6,464	100.1%	100.0%	100.0%	100.0%	100.1%
Nacogdoches City[b]										
White (Non-Hispanic)	2,337	2,292	2,365	1,894	1,472	58.5%	57.0%	55.0%	44.0%	32.6%
Black (Non-Hispanic)	1,580	1,593	1,574	1,585	1,498	39.6%	39.6%	36.6%	36.8%	33.2%
Other Race (Non-Hispanic)	13	15	45	129	212	0.3%	0.4%	1.0%	3.0%	4.7%
Hispanic	63	120	314	701	1,336	1.6%	3.0%	7.3%	16.3%	29.6%
TOTAL	3,993	4,020	4,298	4,309	4,518	100.0%	100.0%	99.9%	100.1%	100.1%
Nacogdoches County[c]										
White (Non-Hispanic)	4,897	5,741	6,425	6,265	5,331	66.7%	71.4%	70.1%	60.6%	50.2%
Black (Non-Hispanic)	2,258	2,061	2,046	2,148	1,912	30.8%	25.6%	22.3%	20.8%	18.0%
Other Race (Non-Hispanic)	17	15	66	215	393	0.2%	0.2%	0.7%	2.1%	3.7%
Hispanic	166	226	632	1,708	2,991	2.3%	2.8%	6.9%	16.5%	28.1%
TOTAL	7,338	8,043	9,169	10,336	10,627	100.0%	100.0%	100.0%	100.0%	100.0%

Table 2 (continued)

Note: Percentages may not total 100.0% due to rounding error. See Appendix for technical information on estimating numbers of Hispanics and non-Hispanic Whites, Blacks, and others.

a NISD enrollment data sources: 1970 estimates are based on 1968, the closest available year for which records were available (Texas Education Agency, 1970); 1980 (Texas Education Agency, 1981); 1990 (Texas Education Agency, 1991); 2000 (Texas Education Agency, 2001); 2010 (Texas Education Agency, 2011)

b Nacogdoches City data sources: 1970 (U.S. Census Bureau, 1973, Tables 28 and 112); 1980 (U.S. Census Bureau, 1982, Table 32); 1990 (U.S. Census Bureau, 1992, Table 61); 2000 (U.S. Census Bureau; Census 2000 Summary File 2; Matrices PCT3 and PCT4; generated by Robert Szafran; using American FactFinder; http://factfinder2.census.gov; 10 March 2014); 2010 (U.S. Census Bureau; Census 2010 Summary File 2; Tables PCT3 and PCT4; generated by Robert Szafran; using American FactFinder; http://factfinder2.census.gov; 10 March 2014)

c Nacogdoches County data sources: 1970 (U.S. Census Bureau, 1973, Tables 35 and 129); 1980 (U.S. Census Bureau, 1982, Table 51); 1990 (U.S. Census Bureau, 1992, Table 54); 2000 (U.S. Census Bureau; Census 2000 Summary File 1; Matrices P13 and PCT12; generated by Robert Szafran; using American FactFinder; http://factfinder2.census.gov; 26 May 2014); 2010 (U.S. Census Bureau; Census 2010 Summary File 1; Tables P12, P13 and PCT12; generated by Robert Szafran; using American FactFinder; http://factfinder2.census.gov; 26 May 2014)

NISD's boundaries correspond to neither the city's nor the county's boundaries. The district extends well beyond the city's limits but well short of the county's boundaries. While most of NISD's enrollment comes from within the city, most of the district lies outside of the city. Nevertheless, comparisons with the 5 through 17 year-old city and county populations, what we shall call the "school-age populations," provide the best available demographic context for understanding changes in NISD enrollment. (Only starting with the 2010 Census has the Census Bureau begun reporting the demographic characteristics of populations by school district. While that 2010 school district-specific census information is useful and will be referenced later in this chapter, by itself it provides little help in documenting changes leading up to 2010.)

As Table 2 shows, the White school-age population in both the city and the county declined starting in the 1990s. The rate of decline in the city was greater than in the county but neither matched the even faster rate of decline from 1990 to 2010 in White enrollment experienced by the district.

The Hispanic school-age population in the city and the county began to rapidly increase in the 1980s and continued to surge through 2010, producing a corresponding rise in Hispanic enrollment in NISD. Growth in NISD's number of Hispanic students parallels and, in fact, slightly exceeds the census-reported growth in the Hispanic school-age population in the city and county—that excess possibly the result of census undercount, better registration and retention of Hispanic children in school, and the establishment of a pre-kindergarten program.

Changes in the Black school-age population like changes in NISD's Black enrollment are modest. There are small decreases in the number of Black school-age children in both the city and the county from 1970 to 2010 but small increases in the number of Black students enrolled in NISD—once again, possibly the result of census undercount, better retention of Black students in school, and the creation of the pre-kindergarten program.

As noted earlier, for the 2010 Census and only for the 2010 Census, NISD's enrollment can be compared not only to the school-age populations of the city and the county but also to the school-age population residing specifically within NISD's boundaries. An analysis of the 5 to 17 year-old population residing within the district in 2010 confirms earlier conclusions based on comparisons with the city and county (U.S. Bureau of the Census 2014). Census data indicates the school-age population residing within the district was 37.4% White, 34.9% Hispanic, 23.6% Black, and 4.1% other races. Compared to these figures, NISD's enrollment (43.0% Hispanic, 29.9% Black, 25.3% White, and 1.9% other races) was more Black, more Hispanic, and substantially less White than the resident school-age population in the district.

SFASU Enrollment and the 18 to 24 Year-Old Population

The period from 1970 to 2010 also saw a dramatic change in the racial/Hispanic composition of SFASU enrollment. While never officially barring Hispanic enrollment, SFASU only formally allowed Black students to enroll starting in the 1960s. Table 3 shows the change in SFASU enrollment. (While the university does not include international students in its racial/Hispanic reporting, international students have never constituted a large share of the student population. In Fall 2010, for example, there were 163 international students out of a total student population of 12,954. See Table 3 opposite page.)

Table 3					
SFA Fall Enrollment for 1970 to 2010					
	Number of Persons				
	1970	1980	1990	2000	2010
	Number of Persons				
SFA Enrollment					
White (Non-Hispanic)	9,377	10,209	11,722	9,109	8,072
Black (Non-Hispanic)	154	433	625	1,485	2,930
Other Race (Non-Hispanic)	42	55	102	187	279
Hispanic	41	184	334	647	1,198
TOTAL	9,614	10,881	12,783	11,428	12,479
	Percent of Enrollment				
SFA Enrollment					
White (Non-Hispanic)	97.5%	93.8%	91.7%	79.7%	64.7%
Black (Non-Hispanic)	1.6%	4.0%	4.9%	13.0%	23.5%
Other Race (Non-Hispanic)	0.4%	0.5%	0.8%	1.6%	2.2%
Hispanic	0.4%	1.7%	2.6%	5.7%	9.6%
TOTAL	99.9%	100.0%	100.0%	100.0%	100.0%

Note: Percentages may not total 100.0% due to rounding error.
Source: SFASU Office of Institutional Research, personal correspondence, 16 December 2014. Numbers as provided are excluding international students and those not reporting race.

Both the number of White students and their percent of the student body have declined strikingly. Whites made up 97.5% of SFASU's student population in 1970 but that decreased to 64.7% in 2010. The actual number of White students peaked in 1990 and then declined. While total enrollment at SFASU dropped during the 1990s and then recovered in the 2000s, White enrollment dropped in the 1990s and continued to drop in the 2000s. Total enrollment at SFASU in 2010 nearly matched total enrollment in 1990 but White enrollment in 2010 was more than 3,600 less than in 1990.

As the White share of enrollment dropped, Black, other race, and Hispanic numbers and shares of enrollment all increased. Each of these increased in both actual numbers and in percent share in every decade, but increases after 1990 are much larger than increases before that year. In 2010, Blacks made up almost one-fourth of the student population and Hispanics almost one-tenth.

Universities do not have officially designated market areas from which they draw students, and SFASU enrolls students not just from nearby areas but from across Texas, other states, and other countries. However, a longstanding observation about SFASU students is that about one-third come from East Texas, about one-third from the Dallas metropolitan

Table 4

18 to 24 Year-Old Population in SFASU's 49 County Market Region for 1970 to 2010

	Number of Persons				
	1970	1980	1990	2000	2010
Dallas Ft Worth Metro Area					
White (Non-Hispanic)	231,653	300,754	274,553	244,353	255,297
Black (Non-Hispanic)	43,869	63,763	69,464	73,789	96,544
Other Race (Non-Hispanic)	3,086	6,633	11,619	29,603	43,205
Hispanic	20,115	41,641	82,483	171,475	207,566
TOTAL	298,723	412,791	438,119	519,220	602,612
East Texas					
White (Non-Hispanic)	49,370	75,029	67,464	67,770	67,918
Black (Non-Hispanic)	15,798	21,813	20,212	19,976	22,268
Other Race (Non-Hispanic)	238	742	741	1,787	2,903
Hispanic	1,883	4,156	6,777	14,347	21,453
TOTAL	67,289	101,740	95,194	103,880	114,542
Houston Galveston Metro Area					
White (Non-Hispanic)	166,128	267,102	192,169	163,081	170,778
Black (Non-Hispanic)	54,802	85,582	80,358	82,765	108,733
Other Race (Non-Hispanic)	2,340	8,980	13,138	29,053	42,780
Hispanic	30,216	73,189	108,231	186,565	244,321
TOTAL	253,486	434,853	393,896	461,464	566,612
Average for Three Regions					
White (Non-Hispanic)					
Black (Non-Hispanic)					
Other Race (Non-Hispanic)					
Hispanic					
TOTAL					

area, and about one-third from the Houston metropolitan area.

Notes: Percents may not total 100.0% due to rounding. See Appendix for technical information on estimating numbers of Hispanics and non-Hispanic Whites, Blacks, and others. Sources: 1970 (U.S. Census Bureau, 1973, Tables 35 and 129); 1980 (U.S. Census Bureau, 1982, Table 45 and 51); 1990 (U.S. Census Bureau, 1992, Table 54); 2000 (U.S. Census Bureau; Census 2000 Summary File 1; Matrices P13 and PCT12; generated by Robert Szafran; using American FactFinder; http://factfinder2.census.gov; 26 May 2014); 2010 (U.S. Census Bureau; Census 2010 Summary File 1; Tables P12, P13 and PCT12; generated by Robert Szafran; using American FactFinder; http://factfinder2.census.gov; 26 May 2014)

	Percent of Population				
	1970	1980	1990	2000	2010
Dallas Ft Worth Metro Area					
White (Non-Hispanic)	77.5%	72.9%	62.7%	47.1%	42.4%
Black (Non-Hispanic)	14.7%	15.4%	15.9%	14.2%	16.0%
Other Race (Non-Hispanic)	1.0%	1.6%	2.7%	5.7%	7.2%
Hispanic	6.7%	10.1%	18.8%	33.0%	34.4%
TOTAL	99.9%	100.0%	100.1%	100.0%	100.0%
East Texas					
White (Non-Hispanic)	73.4%	73.7%	70.9%	65.2%	59.3%
Black (Non-Hispanic)	23.5%	21.4%	21.2%	19.2%	19.4%
Other Race (Non-Hispanic)	0.4%	0.7%	0.8%	1.7%	2.5%
Hispanic	2.8%	4.1%	7.1%	13.8%	18.7%
TOTAL	100.1%	99.9%	100.0%	99.9%	99.9%
Houston Galveston Metro Area					
White (Non-Hispanic)	65.5%	61.4%	48.8%	35.3%	30.1%
Black (Non-Hispanic)	21.6%	19.7%	20.4%	17.9%	19.2%
Other Race (Non-Hispanic)	0.9%	2.1%	3.3%	6.3%	7.6%
Hispanic	11.9%	16.8%	27.5%	40.4%	43.1%
TOTAL	99.9%	100.0%	100.0%	99.9%	100.0%
Average for Three Regions					
White (Non-Hispanic)	72.2%	69.3%	60.8%	49.2%	43.9%
Black (Non-Hispanic)	19.9%	18.9%	19.2%	17.1%	18.2%
OtherRace (Non-Hispanic)	0.8%	1.5%	2.3%	4.6%	5.8%
Hispanic	7.2%	10.3%	17.8%	29.1%	32.1%
TOTAL	100.1%	100.0%	100.1%	100.0%	100.0%

For the present analysis these areas will be treated as a very unofficial market area and will be operationally defined as the 26 counties belonging to either the East Texas or the Deep East Texas Councils of Government, the 14 counties making up the Dallas Fort Worth metropolitan area, and the 9 counties making up the Houston metropolitan area. Table 4 shows how the racial/Hispanic composition of 18 to 24 year-olds in each of these areas changed from 1970 to 2010.

The 18 to 24 year-old population who will be referred to as "young adults" was used because four of every five SFASU students in 2010 were 24 years of age or younger (SFASU, 2011). Looking at young adults in these 49 counties is done simply to put SFASU's changing enrollment into a larger demographic context. It provides a point of comparison but far from a perfect one. SFASU does not have an official recruiting area; and, if it did, it would not be limited to only persons between the ages of 18 and 24; but it would be limited to persons meeting admission requirements which, among other things, include having a high school degree—something many young adults in Texas in 2010 lacked.

Determining the racial/Hispanic composition of SFASU's market area by simply combining these three areas would give too little weight to the East Texas counties whose total population is much smaller than either of the metropolitan areas. The last part of Table 4, therefore, averages the racial and Hispanic composition of the three regions—thereby maintaining the one-third, one-third, and one-third proportions of SFASU's historical enrollment.

Looking at the percentage changes in the averages for the combined three regions, some familiar patterns appear. Whites decline each year as a percent of the young adult population, Blacks essentially maintain a steady share, and Hispanics and persons of other races increase each decade. Looking at the numbers of young adults, Whites increase in the 1970s in all three areas as baby boomers reach young adulthood and decline during the 1980s in all three areas as baby boomers move out of this age range. In Dallas and Houston, the number of White young adults continues to decline through the 1990s but begins to increase again in the 2000s. In East Texas the White decline ends by 1990 but then just plateaus. In all three regions the number of Hispanic young adults increases each decade. The same generally holds for the number of persons of other races. And the number of Black young adults increases in most decades in most regions but at a pace that simply keeps their share of the young adult population approximately constant.In light of these regional changes in the young adult population, SFASU's increased enrollment of Hispanics and persons of other races would seem predictable as would its declining White share of enrollment. Not so predictable until viewed historically are SFASU's increased enrollment of Black young adults despite little growth in the Black young adult population and SFASU's decrease in the actual number of White students—a decrease of greater magnitude than was apparent in any of its recruiting areas. Considering how poor the university's enrollment of Blacks had historically been, increases in Black enrollment at SFASU can be seen as the university becoming more representative of its market area. Conversely, considering how White the university's enrollment had historically been, dramatic decreases in the number of White students, while not likely intended by the university, once again simply moved the university closer to being representative of its market area.

Discussion

The changing demographics of NISD, the city, the county, and the state over the last 40 years have resulted in these entities becoming not more but less similar to one another regarding race and Hispanic status. The city of Nacogdoches is increasingly different from the county as a whole; the county is increasingly different from the state as a whole; and NISD's enrollment is increasingly different from the school-age populations of the city and the county. And despite dramatic changes, differences between SFASU's enrollment and the young adult population in its market area when it comes to race and Hispanic status are as large in 2010 as they were in 1970. These are the conclusions from an examination of changes in a statistic known as the Dissimilarity Index (DI).

The DI is a simple device for comparing two percentage distributions. Computationally, the index represents the percent of cases in one distribution that would have to move to another category in order to make the first percentage distribution identical to the second (Vogt & Johnson, 2011, p. 113). The greater the percentage of cases that would have to move to make the distributions identical, the greater is the dissimilarity between the initial distributions, and the higher is the score of the index. The values for the index range from 0 (complete similarity because the initial distributions are identical) to 100 (complete dissimilarity because the initial distributions do not overlap at all, for example, everyone in the first distribution is White or Black and everyone in the second distribution is other race or Hispanic).

Over these 40 years the city and the county have become less similar. In 1970, the racial/Hispanic composition of the city and the county were quite similar (DI = 3.3); but by 2010, the differences had increased (DI = 11.2). This came about because Blacks in the county were more likely to be living in the city in 2010 than in 1970 while Whites in the county were less likely to be living in the city in 2010 than in 1970.

Over these 40 years the county and the state have become less similar. In 1970 the county was more White, more Black, and less Hispanic than the state (DI = 16.1) and the differences, particularly for Whites and Hispanics, increased by 2010 (DI = 22.6). While the White share of the county's population declined over these forty years, the White share of the state population declined even faster, thereby widening the gap between the county and the state. Conversely, the Hispanic share of the county population increased over these 40 years but not as fast as for the state as a whole, thereby again widening the gap between the county and the state.

The differences between NISD's enrollment and the school-age populations of both the city and the county have grown over the last 40 years. In 1970 NISD's racial/Hispanic enrollment was a pretty good match with the city's school-age population (DI = 5.2) and the county's school-age population (DI = 4.8). That was no longer the case in 2010. While the percent of school-age children in both the city and the county who were White declined sharply from 1970 to 2010, the percent of NISD's enrollment that was White plummeted; and while the percent of school-age children in both the city and the county who were Hispanic rose sharply from 1970 to 2010, the percent of NISD's enrollment that was Hispanic skyrocketed. These differentials made the NISD enrollment in 2010 quite different from the city's school-age population (DI = 13.4) and even more different from the county's school-age population (DI = 26.8). The Census Bureau's district-specific school-age population figures for 2010 support the conclusion of substantial differences between the resident school-age population of the district and NISD's enrollment in 2010 (DI = 14.4).

SFASU's enrollment and the young adult population in its market area differed greatly in 1970 (DI = 25.4) and they continued to differ greatly in 2010 (DI = 26.1). The Black differential between SFASU and its market area diminished markedly from 1970 to 2010 only to be replaced by an even larger Hispanic differential. And since SFASU's dramatic drop in the White share of enrollment only slightly exceeded the drop in the White share of the young adult population in the market area, the White differential between SFASU and its market area was only slightly smaller in 2010 than in 1970.

Conclusion

Certain population trends have been noted again and again in this chapter: growth in the number and percent of Hispanics, growth but to a lesser extent in the number and percent of persons of other races, decreasing number and percent of Whites, and modest growth in the number of Blacks usually just sufficient to maintain their share of the population. The major demographic forces producing these changes are well known: in-migration of Hispanics, higher Hispanic birth rates than Black birth rates, and higher Black birth rates than White birth rates (Migration Policy Institute, 2014; Texas Department of State Health Services, 2012). For Nacogdoches City, out-migration of Whites and in-migration of Blacks has also occurred to produce the large drop in the number of White residents and the sizable increase in the number of Black residents since 1990.

In thinking about Nacogdoches City migration, it is important to remember that while some city migration consists of households moving in or out of the city, SFASU produces much of the city's migration flows. SFASU is a migration engine which regularly brings in and sends out large numbers of young adults of all races. The drop in SFASU White enrollment and the increase in Black enrollment meant that the inflow of Whites to the city decreased while the inflow of Blacks increased. These altered flows are then reflected in the racial and Hispanic composition of the city.

Change in student enrollment at NISD and at SFASU share many similarities: decreasing number and percent of White students, increasing number and percent of Hispanic students, and increasing number and percent of students of other races. For both educational institutions the 1990s appear to be a transition period when White enrollment starts to drop and both Hispanic and other race enrollment increases in magnitude. It is also in the 1990s that Black enrollment at SFASU begins to rapidly grow.

While demographic forces account for much of the change in NISD and SFASU enrollment, demographic forces alone are not the total explanation. Possibilities at the school-district level include increased registration and retention of minority students and increased home-schooling, private schools, and out-of-district transfers by White students. Possibilities at the university level include increased competition among universities for students, state-wide efforts to increase enrollment and retention of historically underrepresented groups, and expanded university admission possibilities through the state's adoption of the common college application and the automatic admission into any state public university for students graduating in the top 10% of their high school class.

References

Gibson, C., & Jung, K. (2002). Historical census statistics on population totals by race, 1790 to 1990, and by Hispanic origin, 1970 to 1990, for the United States, regions, divisions, and states. (U.S. Census Bureau, Population Division, Working Paper No. 56). Washington, DC: U.S. Census Bureau.

Migration Policy Institute. (2014). *State immigration data profiles* (Texas). Retrieved from http://www.migrationpolicy.org/data/state-profiles/state/demographics/TX

Stephen F. Austin State University. (2011). *Fact book, Fall 2010*. Office of Institutional Research. Retrieved from http://www.sfasu.edu/research/docs/fb2010-headcount.pdf

Texas Department of State Health Services. (2012). *2012 natality*. Retrieved from http://www.dshs.state.tx.us/chs/vstat/vs10/nnatal.shtm

Texas Education Agency. (1970). *Annual Statistical Report 1968-69, Part 1* (Bulletin 698). Austin, TX.

Texas Education Agency. (1973). *Annual Statistical Report 1970-71, Part 1* (Bulletin 728). Austin, TX.

Texas Education Agency. (1981). Fall survey of students in Texas public elementary and secondary school districts 1980-81. *Statistical Brief*, Series SB81FSY, December.

Texas Education Agency. (1991). *1990-1991 Academic excellence indicator system district reports: Nacogdoches Independent School District*. Retrieved from http://ritter.tea.state.tx.us/perfreport/aeis/91/district/174904.html

Texas Education Agency. (2001). *2000-2001 Academic excellence indicator system district reports: Nacogdoches Independent School District*. Retrieved from http://ritter.tea.state.tx.us/cgi/sas/broker

Texas Education Agency. (2011). *2010-11 Academic excellence indicator system district reports: Nacogdoches Independent School District*. Retrieved from http://ritter.tea.state.tx.us/perfreport/aeis/2011/district.srch.html

U.S. Census Bureau. (1973). *1970 census of population: Volume 1, Characteristics of the population* (Part 45, Texas). Washington, DC: U.S. Government Printing Office.

U.S. Census Bureau. (1982). *1980 census of population: Volume 1, Characteristics of the population* (PC80-1-45, Texas). Washington, DC: U.S. Government Printing Office.

U.S. Census Bureau. (1992). *1990 census of population: General population characteristics* (CP-1-45, Texas). Washington, DC: U.S. Government Printing Office.

U.S. Census Bureau. (2002). *2000 census of population and housing: Summary population and housing characteristics* (PHC-1-45, Texas). Washington, DC: U.S. Government Printing Office.

U.S. Census Bureau. (2012a). *2010 census of population and housing: Summary population and housing characteristics* (CPH-1-A, Selected Appendices). Washington, DC: U.S. Government Printing Office.

U.S. Census Bureau. (2012b). *2010 census of population and housing: Summary population and housing characteristics* (CPH-1-45, Texas). Washington, DC: U.S. Government Printing Office.

U.S. Census Bureau. (2012c, May 22). Census Bureau releases estimates of undercount and overcount in the 2010 census. U.S. Census Bureau, Office of Public Information, News Release 12-95. Retrieved from http://www.census.gov/newsroom/releases/archives/2010_census/cb12-95.html

U.S. Census Bureau. (2014). Census 2010 Summary File 1; Tables PCT12, 12H, 12I, and 12J; generated by Robert Szafran; using American FactFinder; http://factfinder2.census.gov; 29 July 2014.

Vogt, W. P., & Johnson, R. B.. (2011). *Dictionary of statistics and methodology: A nontechnical guide for the social sciences* (4th ed.). Los Angeles, CA: Sage.

Appendix: Technical Notes

The numbers of Hispanics and non-Hispanic Whites, Blacks, and others residing in Nacogdoches City, Nacogdoches County, other Texas counties, and Texas must sometimes be derived from other published figures. This is particularly the case for small geographic areas, earlier censuses, and limited age groups. The racial and Hispanic enrollment in NISD in 1970 also required indirect estimation. This appendix describes the procedures used in those cases.

1970 NISD Enrollment: Neither TEA nor NISD were able to provide racial and Hispanic enrollment numbers for the district for 1970. The closest year to 1970 for which TEA did report Black and White enrollments by district was 1968 (TEA, 1970). Since the total NISD enrollment of 4,683 in 1968 closely matched the total NISD enrollment of 4,643 in 1970 (TEA, 1973), 1968 figures are used as estimates for the unavailable 1970 figures. The TEA (1970) reported there were 1,665 Black students in the district in 1968 and 3,018 White students; however, the White total would have included Hispanic and other race students. In 1980 the ratio of Hispanic students in NISD to Hispanic 5 to 17 year-olds in the city was 44:120 and the ratio of other race students in NISD to other race 5 to 17 year-olds in the city was 17:15. Using 1970 Census reports of the racial and Hispanic composition of 5 to 17 year-olds and assuming those 1980 ratios were approximately the same in 1970, NISD in 1970 would be estimated to have 23 Hispanic students and 14 students of other races. That would reduce the number of White students to 2,981.

1970 Census, Hispanic Status: 1970 Census reports of number of Hispanics are estimates based on samples of the population and thus subject to a greater margin of error than reports based on later censuses. The 1970 Census directly asked 5% of individuals if they were of Hispanic origin, 15% of individuals what the primary language spoken within their household was, and, for that same 15%, if they had what was judged to be a Hispanic surname. 1970 Census publications usually report an estimate of the number of Hispanic persons in a population based on the number of persons having either a Spanish surname or reporting Spanish to be the primary language spoken in their household, and that is what is used for the tables in this chapter.

1970 Census, Non-Hispanic Whites, Blacks, and Others: 1970 Census publications did not report numbers of non-Hispanics by race. These publications simply reported numbers of Whites, numbers of Blacks, and numbers of persons of other races. Persons who based on surname or primary language spoken within the household were judged to be Hispanic were simply included in those numbers. Estimating the 1970 Census numbers of non-Hispanic Whites, non-Hispanic Blacks, and non-Hispanic persons of other races for the tables in this chapter was done in the following way: Because the Census Bureau (1982, Appendix B) reported that nationally 93% of persons of Hispanic origin either self-classified themselves racially as White or were reclassified as White based on 1970 Census rules, the numbers of non-Hispanic Whites in 1970 reported for all tables in this chapter are the number of Whites reported by the 1970 Census minus the number of Hispanics. The numbers of non-Hispanic Blacks in 1970 and non-Hispanic persons of other races in 1970 are the unadjusted numbers of Blacks and persons of other races reported in the 1970 Census. This slightly underestimates the number of non-Hispanic Whites and slightly overestimates the number of non-Hispanic Blacks and persons of other races.

1970 Census, 5 to 17 Year-Olds and 18 to 24 Year-Olds: 1970 Census publications reported by age the number of Hispanics and the numbers of Whites, Blacks, and persons of other races for Nacogdoches City and for 27 of the counties (including Nacogdoches County) in SFA's recruiting region. With this information, the number of non-Hispanic Whites, Blacks, and persons of other races by age could be estimated by subtracting the Hispanic number from the White total and leaving the Black and other total unchanged (see previous paragraph). For the other 22 counties in SFA's recruiting region, the numbers of Whites, Blacks, and persons of other races were reported by age but, because there were fewer than 400 Hispanics in the county, neither the number of Hispanics by age nor the total number of Hispanics was reported. For the purpose of estimating the Hispanic share of SFA's entire 18-24 year-old recruiting area population, it was assumed that each of these 22 counties had 35 Hispanics between the ages of 18 and 24. The number 35 was based on the assumption that each of these 22 counties had a total Hispanic population of 200 (we know it was less than 400) and 17.5% of those were 18 to 24 years old (which was the percent of the Hispanic population in the state between the ages of 18 and 24 in 1970. While these assumptions are arbitrary, in the end they are of only negligible importance since these 22 counties had generally small populations and together represented only a small share of the 18 to 24 year-old population in SFA's recruiting region,

1980 Census, 5 to 17 Year-Olds and 18 to 24 Year-Olds: 1980 Census publications reported by age the number of Hispanics and the numbers of non-Hispanic Whites, non-Hispanic Blacks, and non-Hispanic persons of other races for 33 of the counties (including Nacogdoches County) in SFA's recruiting region. For Nacogdoches City and for the other 16 counties in SFA's recruiting region, census publications reported by age the number of Hispanics and by age the number of Whites, Blacks, and persons of other races but not by age the number of non-Hispanic Whites, Blacks, and persons of other races. (Unlike the 1970 Census, the 1980 Census did not reclassify as White persons saying their race was Hispanic.) Because the Census Bureau (1982, Appendix B) reported that nationally 56% of persons of Hispanic origin reported their race as White and 40% reported their race as Hispanic which would have placed them in the category "other races," the following procedure was used to estimate for Nacogdoches City the number of 5 to 17 year-old and for those 16 counties the number of 18 to 24 year-old non-Hispanic Whites, Blacks, and persons of other races: the number of non-Hispanic Whites was the number of Whites reported by the census minus 60% of the number of Hispanics and the number of non-Hispanic persons of other races was the number of persons of other races reported by the census minus 40% of the number of Hispanics. The numbers of non-Hispanic Blacks for 1980 was the unadjusted numbers of Blacks reported in the 1980 census. This slightly underestimates the number of non-Hispanic Whites and slightly overestimates the number of non-Hispanic Blacks.

1990 Census, 5 to 17 Year-Olds and 18 to 24 Year-Olds: For counties and cities 1990 Census publications reported by age the number of Hispanics, Whites, Blacks, persons of other races, and the number of non-Hispanic Whites but not by age the number of non-Hispanic Blacks or the number of non-Hispanic persons of other races. For the tables in this chapter, the number of non-Hispanic persons of other races in 1990 was estimated by reducing the total number of persons of other races by the number of Hispanics not reporting their race as White. The numbers of non-Hispanic Blacks in 1990 was estimated to be the number of Blacks reported in the 1990 census. This slightly underestimates the number of non-Hispanic persons of other races and slightly overestimates the number of non-Hispanic Blacks.

2000 and 2010 Censuses, Multiple Racial Ancestry: Starting with the 2000 Census, individuals could self-identify as being of more than one race. Thus far, relatively few individuals make use of that option; however, those non-Hispanics that do are classified as "non-Hispanic other race" for the tables in this chapter.

Integration and Re-segregation: Voices from the Past and Present

By: Dr. D. Michelle Williams

Sixty years after Brown versus Board of Education and 45 years after Nacogdoches was forced to integrate its schools, schools across the country are becoming increasingly more segregated. At the peak of integration in 1988, 43.5 percent of African American students attended schools with a majority of White students (Orfield & Lee, 2004). In 2001, that number had dropped to 30.3 percent, the lowest since 1968. Since 1991, 38 districts have sought to have segregation orders lifted. These districts were no longer obligated to maintain a plan to continue the desegregation efforts achieved. All but four of the 38 districts have shown evidence of re-segregation (Holley, 2005).

Financially poor White students and students of Color who attend racially segregated schools often receive a lower quality of education. Black (2011) noted desegregation as the most important policy to improve outcomes for historically marginalized students. Black lists the following disadvantages: 1) lower quality and unequal access to curriculum, 2) fewer high quality teachers, 3) lack of exposure and influence of middle and upper class peers, and 4) long term lowered achievement. Schools with high concentrations of students of Color and financially poor students are a direct reflection of community demographics.

There are many reasons why we have witnessed racially and economically charged re-segregation in the United States. Often, White families move from urban to suburban areas for access to better jobs, schools, and opportunities. Therefore, urban schools are left with high concentrations of marginalized students. The lifting of segregation orders has allowed districts to ease efforts to force racially motivated integration in schools. In doing so, social re-segregation has occurred as students are assigned to neighborhood schools. Similar to urban environments, rural cities have witnessed the same type of economic and racial segregation. This trend has been evident in Nacogdoches. Over the past 15 years the percent of students of Color in Nacogdoches Independent School District (NISD) has remained significantly higher than the population of Nacogdoches (Szafran, 2015). This trend can also be attributed to students attending private schools throughout the area and the excessive number of smaller, primarily White, rural districts within a 25-mile radius.

In this chapter, I examine the perspectives of African Americans who lived through the integration of schools in the Nacogdoches area. As I read and/or listened to their stories, it is clear that the forced integration had both positive and negative implications for African American students. I reviewed the African American Heritage Project Interviews (AAHP, 2010) and conducted interviews of my own to hear the perspective of the people who were most affected by the integration of Nacogdoches schools.

Common Themes

A number of themes emerged as I examined transcripts of interviews with African Americans throughout East Texas concerning their experiences with integration. The first and most obvious theme is that the integration of public schools led to a better education. While those who attended all Black schools reported receiving a good education prior to 1970, they also acknowledged a lack of resources and opportunities compared to the education obtained the White schools. With the integration of the schools, there was also a sense of fear and loss. The African American schools were the center of a close-knit community. The parents, students, and teachers built relationships beyond the school environment. Additionally, there was fear concerning the new primarily White environment. Schools were integrated with little input or preparation from those involved in the transition.

Fear

African American students were both excited about the prospects of a better education and fearful of the unknown as schools were integrated in 1970. One student expressed it this way, "For me personally, it was a rude awakening because I wanted to press to the other side, but I was nervous. I knew that my education was probably not up to par, but I was intent on making it no matter what" (AAHP, 2010, Rison). Another student noted, "There were a bunch of scared Black folks, let me tell you. We were very, very afraid" (AAHP, 2010, Rison). Much of this fear was the fear of the unknown. There had been little preparation prior to integration, and the students did not know what to expect. One of the first African Americans to attend Nacogdoches High School shared, "We were really not accepted into to the school with open arms, you know? The majority of us really did not want to go to NHS because of all the riots that were happening around the country" (Taylor, 2014, p. 16). The prevailing attitude of the times created tension and anxiety. Marian Upshaw commented that the history of segregation and Jim Crow was deeply engrained. He shared, "The mind is a powerful thing. So we were still enslaved by that attitude that was instilled in us for all our lives." However, the opportunity of a quality education was the driving force for many African Americans as they began the journey of an integrated education.

Quality Education

Even when it was inaccessible and illegal, African Americans have historically valued education. It has been documented that education was viewed as a pathway to psychological and religious freedom (Cornelius, 1991). The plaintiffs in the *Brown versus Board of Education* (1954) case were motivated by a deep desire for quality education. Segregated schools were obviously not equal. African American schools had limited resources and used the books and resources discarded by the White schools. In the late 1960s, Nacogdoches allowed parents to send their children to the school of their choice. Some African American parents and children chose to attend the White schools seeking access to better education and more resources. Others preferred to stay in the all Black school with less resources. Verdis Daniels was one of those students who attended a White school prior to 1970. His mother reported: "He loved Raguet, and the teachers loved him. They knew what he could do and how smart he was." Verdis shared, "The teachers were very supportive and pushed me academically" (Daniels, 2015, p. 108). In 1970, school choice was no longer an option in Nacogdoches due to court ordered school integration. Daniels reported that while he experienced academic success at Nacogdoches High School, he felt socially isolated from his peers.

While African American parents and children were fearful, they looked at integration as an opportunity to receive a better education. Mr. Neal, a former NISD administrator, stated "my parents sat us down before going and said, 'look, it is not going to be easy, but the only way to do well in life is to get an education. We are sending you over there to mind, be respectful, and learn. Get your high school diploma.'"

Sense of Community

There was a strong sense of family and community in the African American community prior to integration. Archie Rison (AAHP, 2010) described his segregated school as a "close knit community" with "a feeling of unity." E. J. Campbell High School on Shawnee Street was the hub of the African American community in Nacogdoches. Parents were actively involved in the school and community. Teachers and parents knew each other well and socialized outside of school. The teachers attended the same churches as the parents and students. "You couldn't cut-up in class because you knew that the teacher would tell your mama and daddy" (AAHP, 2010).

When schools were integrated in 1970, this sense of community was lost. Teachers did not know the parents of many of the new Black students. Even though the school was integrated, racial groups were still segregated within the community. Whites socialized with Whites, and Blacks socialized with Blacks. While some more recent graduates refer to individual teachers who created a caring classroom environment, the former unity experienced in the all Black school has been lost. This is validated by Ladson-Billings (2000) who stated, "Community access and involvement, trust between teachers and parents, and concern and caring for students were all hallmarks of these schools where the needs of African students were paramount" (p. 207). If school integration is to be successful, creating a caring community is essential.

Relationships

A number of authors have written about the importance of caring relationships to children's success in school (Kaplin & Owings, 2000; Kohn, 2005; Noddings, 1995, 2005). African Americans in Nacogdoches shared stories that demonstrate the importance of caring teachers to their success in school. Those who attended segregated schools spoke of the close relationships in those schools. One former E.J. Campbell student stated, "It was very, very, very good. All the teachers knew the parents really well, and everyone was close. The teachers were nice, and you knew that they loved you and cared about you. Back then, you would listen to the adults." Parental involvement was high. "You had to get your lessons because if one of these teachers picked up the phone or wrote a note home to your parent, then boy, when you got home. They [parents] were on you. Like I said, they [teachers] were concerned about you, and they cared about you because they knew what you were going to be faced with [as an African American student]." One person stated, "Teachers were more like parents. What they said was the Bible." Overall, those who attended all Black schools felt that teachers taught students to care about each other and demonstrated how to help and respect others. School was centered on caring relationships.

Students from both segregated and integrated schools were consistent in speaking about the importance of caring relationships. Speaking of her English teacher a graduate shared "She didn't just teach me about literature. She taught me about life. We still share a relationship to this day" (Taylor, 2014, p. 12). Similarly, a former E.J. Campbell student reported "E.J. Campbell may not have had the most modern technology for that time, but we were educated and we were loved. The campus, the teachers, the students, and the parents were all family. It wasn't a stressful environment" (Taylor, 2014, p. 17). Another spoke of a teacher who saw his potential and challenged him. He shared that he did not expect to graduate, but this teacher refused to let him give up. She told him, "I am not going to accept this work from you. You can do better. I want you to do better." He began making A's and B's, went to college, became a teacher, and later a school administrator. These stories illustrate the impact of caring teachers who create a safe haven for students based on mutual trust and respect (Knowles & Brown, 2000).

School districts face many challenges to providing quality educational experiences for their students. Nacogdoches ISD continues to struggle with low-test scores, high staff turnover, deteriorating buildings, and two recent failed bond issues. School leaders strive to provide a quality education for all while patrons voice concern about issues such as school safety, test scores, and the achievement gap. The importance of building relationships with students and parents is as crucial today as it was in the past. NISD must find effective strategies to create a sense of community that many African Americans feel was lost when the schools integrated.

Hope

While the statistics about re-segregation provided earlier in this chapter are discouraging, it is important to recognize the accomplishments that have been made. In 2008, the United States elected its first African American president, Barack Obama. On the sixtieth anniversary of *Brown versus Board of Education*, First Lady, Michelle Obama, challenged the 2014 graduates of Topeka Public Schools to continue the work that was started in 1954.

> The truth is that *Brown vs. Board of Education* is not
> just about our history, it's about our future.
> Because while that case was handed down 60 years ago,
> Brown is still being decided every single day -- not just
> in our courts and schools, but in how we live our lives.
> Now, our laws may no longer separate us based on our skin
> color, but nothing in the Constitution says we have
> to eat together in the lunchroom, or live together
> in the same neighborhoods.

> There's no court case against believing in stereotypes
> or thinking that certain kinds of hateful jokes
> or comments are funny.
> So the answers to many of our challenges today
> can't necessarily be found in our laws.
> These changes also need to take place in our hearts
> and in our minds.
>
> (Obama, 2014)

After sharing his story of attending segregated schools and going to the back of the diner to pick up a hamburger, one African American man who attended both segregated and integrated schools exclaimed,

> I look at the schools now and how they've changed. When I walk in the stores now and see how they've changed. I was telling my wife look at the commercials on TV. We thought we would never, in this area, will see a Black man with a White woman or a Black woman with a White man. But now you walk into the campus and look at the beautiful picture you have. You have the mixed marriages. The kids look different; you see this melting pot. I get excited when I see that because that's the way it should be, and that's the way God wanted it to be. All of us working together.

The hope and future of our schools is in the hearts of the children who are now attending school. Adults in the lives of today's children have the responsibility to teach and model respect and care for others. These lessons are best learned through interactions and experiences with diversity in schools and other community settings.

Conclusion

While many acknowledge that schools are becoming increasing segregated, there are few suggested solutions. Black (2011) suggests that legal incentives be offered to districts that develop plans to sustain integration of schools. The answer is not likely to come from the courts as recent cases have upheld local control of assigning students to schools (Black, 2011). He suggests a call for recommitment by those involved in education. Community partnerships such as the one described by Childress (2015) between Austin Heights Baptist Church and Zion Hill Baptist church are examples of efforts to improve relationships between diverse groups in the community. The Office of Multicultural Affairs at Stephen F. Austin State University has been instrumental in promoting relationships among diverse populations in Nacogdoches. The group has sponsored a number of activities to build community such as a peace rally, Martin Luther King Day of Service, Tunnel of Oppression, and others. Recently, a diverse group of concerned citizens joined together to support the Nacogdoches school district to promote the bond issue and provide support for students and teachers in the schools. A number of other groups such as The Organization of Faith, Education, and Community, and Diversifying Nacogdoches work to promote acceptance and harmony among diverse groups in Nacogdoches. These efforts are just a beginning to building a caring community where persons of Color feel like they belong and that they do not have to fear of being rejected or discriminated against due to race.

Marian, a community leader, told a story to illustrate the need to recommit to integration. He told the story of a dog walking through the neighborhood. He sees another dog with a bone and immediately fights the dog and retrieves the bone. The dog continues along with the bone in his mouth, and some other dogs notice the bone. They jump on him and take that bone. He continues by stating "The thing you had to fight to get, you must fight to keep." That is true with integration as well. Martin Luther King, Jr. and others fought for the rights that African Americans now enjoy. Marian asks "Who is working on it now?" We must continue to fight to keep what others worked hard to win.

References

African American Heritage Project (AAHP), (2010). East Texas African American Oral Histories, East Texas Research Center, retrieved from http://www.sfasu.edu/heritagecenter/422.asp.

Black, D. W. (2011). Voluntary desegregation, resegregation, and the hope for equal educational opportunity. *Human Rights 38*(4), 2-5.

Brown v. Board of Education, 347 U.S. 483 (1954).

Childress, K. (2015). Confessing whiteness. In D. M. Williams & B. L. Fox (Eds.) *Nacogdoches: Integration and Segregation, Then and Now*. Nacogdoches, TX: SFA Press.

Cornelius, J. D. (1991). *When I can read my title clear: Literacy, slavery, and religion in the antebellum south*. Columbia, SC: University of South Carolina Press.

Daniels, V. (2015). My Story: Experiencing the racial environment of the 60s and 70s in Nacogdoches, Texas. In D. M. Williams & B. L. Fox (Eds.) *Nacogdoches: Integration and Segregation, Then and Now*. Nacogdoches, TX: SFA Press.

Holley, D. R. (2005). Is Brown dying? Exploring re segregation in our public schools. *New York School Law Review*, 1, 1085-1107.

Kim, J., & Sunderman, G. L. (2004). Does NCLB provide good choices for students in low performing schools? Cambridge, MA: The Civil Rights Project at Harvard University.

Kaplan, L. S., & Owings, W. A. (2000). Helping kids feel safe, valued and competent. *The Education Digest*, 66(3), 24-28.

Knowles, T., & Brown, D. F. (2000). *What every middle school teacher should know*. Westerville, OH: National Middle School Association.

Kohn, A. (2005). Unconditional teaching. *Educational Leadership, 63*(1), 20-24.

Ladson-Billings, G. (2000). Fighting for our lives: Preparing teachers to teach African American students. *Journal of Teacher Education*, 51(3), 206-214. Retrieved from http://www.fredonia.edu/pdc/keynote/Fighting For Our Lives.pdf

Noddings, N. (1995). Teaching themes of care. *Phi Delta Kappan, 76*(9), 675-679.

Noddings, N. (2005). Identifying and responding to needs in education. *Cambridge Journal of Education, 35*(2), 147-159.

Obama, M. (2014, May 16). First Lady Michelle Obama addresses senior appreciation day in Topeka, Kansas.

Orfield, G., & Lee, C. (2004). Brown at 50: Kings dream or Plessy's Nightmare? *The Civil Rights Project*, Harvard University.

Szafran, R. (2015). The changing racial and Hispanic composition of Nacogdoches and its educational institutions. In D. M. Williams & B. L. Fox (Eds.) *Nacogdoches: Integration and Segregation, Then and Now*. Nacogdoches, TX: SFA Press.

Taylor, B. (2014). History of the Nacogdoches public school system, Unpublished paper for ELE 352, Stephen F. Austin State University.

Paradise Lost

By: Dr. Osaro E. Airen, Mr. Justin Ikpo,
Ms. Kim Foli, and Ms. Alisha Hall

E.J. Campbell (Before Integration)

The wave of integration hit Nacogdoches schools in a significant way in the late 1960s and early 1970s. Before the surge of changes rushed through classrooms, both Whites and African Americans in the Nacogdoches community were educated very differently. Former students of E.J. Campbell High School, the town's African American high school, carry their experiences of youth with them to this day. These experiences of youth, communal involvement, and education in a changing United States of America, echo through their lives and continue to pave their futures. It is said that it takes a village to raise a child. Three former E.J. Campbell High School students: Reverend Leonard Sweat of St. James Baptist Church, Reverend Don Mills of Little Zion Baptist Church and Mr. Jimmy Weaver, all felt this to be true and shared their experiences with this concept.

Foundations

"We were incorporated with the idea that you need to take care of the next person and not be so selfish," Sweat said. In the eyes of Sweat, Mills, and Weaver, most of their peers were cut from the same cloth. Many of whom did not have much.

Everybody back then was poor," said Mills. "Nobody had a lot of money. We were just living in a neighborhood where everybody shared everything. So we wouldn't classify it as poverty." In the poorer African American communities, everyone exchanged and contributed what they could to ensure the success of others. Neighborhoods were seen as villages, and friends and neighbors were seen as siblings.

Regardless of whether they were your own kids, nieces and nephews or just a friend, if you were hungry, you were going to eat — simple as that," Weaver said. "We knew all of our neighbors from the end of the street to the other end of the street." These significant lessons of community support led to a strong foundation of morals within the lives of many students' which was also found within the walls of E.J. Campbell High School.

E.J. Campbell High School

E.J. Campbell High School became a beacon for African American students in Nacogdoches. A place where students, teachers, and parents all interacted regularly like a family—in every sense of the word.

It was a family environment, but most of all, they [teachers] showed us the 'right way' and would not let us fail," said Sweat. "Each teacher knew us by name, and all-in-all, we got a sense that they cared about us so much." Mills understood that his teachers had high expectations academically and behaviorally. This expectation was supported not only by parents, but also the student body.

"They [teachers] demanded respect and our parents demanded that we gave them respect," Mills said. "It was 'yes ma'am and no ma'am' and any time we didn't obey, our mother and father would be there to back them up." School administrators also held their students and teachers to a high standard. The firm attitude resonated its way all the way from the school offices to the school hallways. Mills recalled a former principal of his named Mr. Simon, who was nicknamed "Wolf" for his intimidating presence. Wolf was known for his sharp, professional demeanor.

"Everyone was fearful of Wolf because he didn't play," said Mills. "Nobody wanted to see [him] because he would get you straight." However, these constant factors and the inability to cut corners pushed students to new academic heights regardless of the adversities they faced.

Crossing Hurdles

African American students at E.J. Campbell dealt with many adversities throughout each regular school year. Significant differences between White and African American schools created challenges for students and teachers.

"What they call 'at-risk' was normal in our days," said Mills, referring to current at-risk standards of the school systems of today. "There was no such thing as 'at-risk.' They didn't even use that term."

E.J. Campbell faculty members knew that African American students had fewer resources than White students in Nacogdoches. From school supplies to textbooks, African American students remained on an uneven playing field. White schools often passed down outdated textbooks that were ragged and defaced to the schools that housed African American students. Despite the disadvantages, teachers at E.J. Campbell used what they had to unlock the fullest potential of their students.

We didn't have the best books in the world," said Weaver. "You know with us, we didn't have a lot back then but our teachers made sure that we knew what was in those books."

Mills agreed. Recalling that his class was tested every day to make sure that he and his classmates not only understood the material but could also comprehend it and use it effectively. "We very seldom got brand new books," he said. "But they [teachers] drilled success in your mind, and they made you know that you were somebody important enough to be concerned about that they wanted to see you succeed."

Class time was filled with rigorous memorization and application exercises. "They made us remember things we did in our heads," said Weaver. "We didn't take any true or false tests. Everything we took was completion. You had to fill it in."

In their teachers' eyes, progress and success went hand-in-hand. And parents responded to it well. "We were not exposed to the problems that our parents had to deal with on a daily basis," said Sweat. "They would not bring that burden down on us as children. Their goal for us was to get a good education.

During Integration

It was the Fall of 1970 when Nacogdoches Independent School District (ISD) finally fully integrated its high school. The term "finally" is used in reference to the length of time Nacogdoches ISD waited to desegregate its schools. Nacogdoches ISD waited nearly 16 years after the Brown v. Board of Education ruling to integrate Nacogdoches High School. In 1954, Brown v. Board of Education overturned the 1896 Plessy v. Ferguson case and determined that the "separate but equal" ruling was unlawful. Brown v. Board of Education ruling let it be known that the segregated educational system was systematically unjust and did not provide students of Color with the same education as their White counterparts.

From 1965-1969, prior to the eventual integration, Nacogdoches ISD gave students the opportunity to choose whether to remain at E.J. Campbell High School or go to Nacogdoches High School (Stephen F. Austin State University, N.D.). The decision was quite easy for a majority of E.J. Campbell students due to the fact that they felt comfortable and cared for at E.J. Campbell, and also because they did not feel welcomed at Nacogdoches High School. As Weaver stated, "As far as the integration process, when it all happened, it was like, we didn't want to go over there because we knew they didn't want us over there, but we had to accept the fact that in order for us to go to school we had to go over there." Students wanted to remain at the school where they knew they were treated like family and nurtured by their teachers and school administrators. The students, though, were left without a choice and knew that if they wanted to graduate with a high school diploma, they had to go to Nacogdoches High School. As Weaver said, "we went with the idea that we were going to try to make the best of two worlds."

Once students arrived at Nacogdoches High School, they faced hardships that nobody prepared them for. Students of Color were greeted by a school that was integrated by word only and—in their opinion—teachers, students and administrators did not want them there. As Weaver said,

> There were a lot of hardships. We had to get acclimated to the students, to the teachers and basically, you know, we were integrated but it still was Black—White because all the Blacks sat together and all the Whites sat together. All my friends were Black and all their friends were White. And we never could really mix because nobody knew how to talk to one another.

Thus, the transition to Nacogdoches High School was rather difficult. As Sweat stated,

> The biggest problem was the transition period. Now you had, for a couple of years, you had freedom of choice. It was the choice of the parents to send the kid to Nacogdoches High, but the majority chose not to. But then when it did integrate we had to come. It wasn't a smooth transition because like I said, we didn't know how to communicate…it wasn't talked about.

Mills followed Sweat by stating:

> They never discussed it, they never. I mean in the school meeting they never talked about how we were going to integrate the schools. We didn't talk about the Black methods and the methods we have here (E.J. Campbell). They never talked about that. They just said you're going to be going to Nacogdoches High School. I didn't go. I finished before the school integrated, but I was there to hear and see the repercussion of it. They just closed E.J. Campbell up and turned that gym, the best basketball gym in the district, turned that to the mechanical school.

The transition to Nacogdoches High School was even more difficult for Sweat and Weaver when their former E.J. Campbell school administrators and teachers did not follow them to their new school. As Weaver stated,

> The people we looked up to, the principals and teachers and all those people that were very very important in our lives. When we went to Nacogdoches, instead of having people that we saw as role models they weren't up here anymore, they were down here (demoted). And we're looking at that because we're used to seeing those people at the top. We respected those people and all of a sudden they dropped.

Sweat, Weaver, and their classmates were also not prepared for the level of racism and hate they would encounter once they arrived at Nacogdoches High School as well as the lack of support they received from school administrators. As Weaver acknowledged, "one of the biggest things I remember we were eating lunch off campus one day, and a man drove up a pulled a .30-.30 Winchester on us, and we all ran back to the school and let the people at the school know what happened. They didn't do anything about it." As a result of the incident and the lack of support the students received, Weaver said that he and several other students, "boycotted school the rest of that day, we just walked out." The students simply wanted to feel as if their lives mattered and wanted, "some kind of protection, some, 'we belong,'" as Weaver stated.

In addition to the lack of support the former students received, they were forced to acknowledge the painful fact that everything they and their predecessors achieved at E.J. Campbell would never be recognized by Nacogdoches High School. Once they arrived at Nacogdoches High School, it was as if E.J. Campbell never existed. "And as far as things back at E.J. Campbell, it's like there is no E.J. Campbell," Weaver expressed. The disregard for the achievements of former E.J. Campbell students was quite upsetting with Weaver stating that it, "made me feel very very bad, negative, because we had a whole lot of history, you know preserved history, so people can know where they came from." Sweat also stated that:

> We all had something that they couldn't take away, we all had sports jackets and things like that, and those were material things but in our eyes those were the things that we earned with our hard work in the sport that we played. Not only in the sports, but there were a lot of academic awards. Then you get to Nacogdoches High, and it was like all that didn't mean anything.

In addition, Mills stated:

> I feel like E. J. Campbell's legacy was a part of a formal genocide to do away with the history and the memory of E.J. Campbell High School as though it didn't exist. They know it existed, but they say let's not put it as a part of history. So it's a repeated process of the cultural problems and racial problems that we had. A lot of great things were done at E.J. Campbell, but it was thrown out. A lot of accomplishments were made but it was not remembered.

Mills believed that if Nacogdoches High School closed and the students were required to, instead, attend E.J. Campbell, things would have been different. As he expressed, "I believe that this school district and our relationships in Nacogdoches would be better had Nacogdoches High School joined E.J. Campbell other than E.J. Campbell joining Nacogdoches High School." He added:

> The attitude that we were taught, the curriculum that we taught, and the principles that the teacher used was for children. They taught us to love all children no matter what color or advantages they had or disadvantage. We were taught to love people from our home and then it fed over to our school. We weren't taught to hate White people. Many of the White people's children were taught to dislike Black people. Now it was a problem with me for you being prejudice towards Black people when Black people helped raise you and your parents. Because most of these people my age were raised by Black housekeepers. They raised those children; a lot of White parents didn't even raise their children. They love their nanny more than they did their momma. I believe that the principles, the love that was taught at E.J. Campbell would've made a difference in our community because E. J. Campbell. The village of E. J. Campbell would've accepted the people coming to the Black community rather than the White people accepting the Black people coming into their community. It would've been a great transition.

The former students know that their paradise also known as E.J. Campbell High School, has now been lost in history. Their legacy and their achievements have been thrown away as if their former beloved school never existed. Even though their past accomplishments have been dismantled, Sweat and Weaver wanted it to be known that they were not just students that attended E J. Campbell High School but members of the last group of students to attend the school as well as the first group of students to formally integrate Nacogdoches High School. As Weaver said,

> Well my thing is, back then we were 17 and 18 year old kids, and it was a lot of things happening. Today, my mentality is I'm a part of history. I'm a part of history. I'm a part of history due to the fact that I helped to integrate Nacogdoches High. I'm part of history because I was the last class officially at E. J. Campbell, so I look at things as history now as being a part of history.

After Integration

The hallways G.W. Neal now walks down at Nacogdoches ISD are a far cry from the two-room African American school he attended as a youth in Central Heights. Today, there are White students, African American students, Latin@/Hispanic American students and Asian American students, all learning together under one roof. There are opportunities to play sports and compete. There are opportunities for scholarships, for making college plans, or going to a trade school. There are opportunities to succeed.

But despite these improvements, the now-integrated schools of Nacogdoches have underlying problems rooted in a society that is still, in many ways, segregated. To Neal, the biggest problem African American students face today is a lack of high expectations and an overdose of sympathy. "I think the major thing that has hurt us has been the loss of expectation," he said.

> Our African American teachers demanded performance. When we moved over and integrated, we lost that. They have this sympathy for us. 'Oh poor G.W. He lives in a little house over there, and his parents can't do this or that. I'm not going to give him as much. I'm just going to give him so many words.' That really hurt us. The way for us to get ahead in integration is to demand performance, and to have high expectations. It's Ok to have empathy and to try to understand, but high expectations have been lost. We've gotten behind because of that.

At the root of this problem is a lack of understanding that many White teachers have of their African American students.

> Building relationships has been a challenge for the teachers in integration—the White teachers—have to build a relationship with African American students," he said. "We come from different cultures. We come from a hard-working culture. Language is a little different, and so building relationships has been a problem for our teachers.

Neal, who integrated in Central Heights when he was going into ninth grade, had a different educational experience than African American students today. His two-room schoolhouse had two teachers. One taught kindergarten through fourth grade, and the other taught fifth grade through eighth grade. About five children made up each grade, and each grade sat in their own row. The teacher would move from row to row, switching subjects and grade levels. And when Neal was finished with his studies, he would listen to what the older kids were learning, helping to prepare him for future lessons.

The books Neal received as a student were older, hand-me-downs from the White schools, many with pages torn out and missing. On the first day of class, the first order of business was to take their new eraser and erase the derogatory descriptions of African Americans that had been penciled into the books. But despite all this, Neal said his teachers made sure their students' education was up to par. "It was a wonderful experience," he said.

Neal's parents were mostly uneducated. His mother had a sixth grade education, but his father could not read or write.

"Our teachers had high expectations of us," Neal said. "They knew they had the support of our parents, because our parents wanted us to have a better education. To do better in society, we needed a better education. They loved us and worked us hard and provided an opportunity for us to do better."

If a student disrespected a teacher or acted out in class, mom and dad would know by dinnertime. And that's something Neal said has gone away from modern education. Parental involvement has decreased. Families have changed, and children are falling through the cracks.

"I think really because of lack of high expectations with our teachers today—not all, but most--we're behind," he said.

Neal had a few teachers at Central Heights, after integration that demanded performance.

"I remember, because this teacher demanded performance out of all of us, I was one of those that it stayed with me," he said. "I began to do better and perform better." Neal is saddened by modern terms used to describe children who "don't mind."

"There's a term called Opposition Defiant Disorder, meaning kids don't have a lot of reasoning and don't respect authority," he said. "Well, I may have had that a couple times when I was small, but Daddy took care of that pretty quick."

Neal, who recently came out of retirement temporarily to serve as interim principal at Raguet Elementary School, said today's teachers face new challenges.

"The young teachers today struggle with working with African American students," he said. "They really don't understand them. What I mean by understanding, you have to build relationships with them. They have to know that you trust them. They have to know that you really care."

Neal said the teachers who cared for him and demanded his best were the ones who made a difference in his life. And while young, typically White, teachers may care for their students, they're not sure how to relate. He's had many conversations over the years with teachers, offering them advice and sometimes even taking them to those African American communities so they can see the culture first hand.

"I'll take one teacher, for instance," he said. "A third grade White teacher, veteran teacher, struggled. She said 'Mr. Neal, I don't understand why this child does not bring a paper or pencil to school,' so I said, 'let's go visit the home.' We got in my old truck, and we drove to the neighborhood. Before we could get in the house, there was people standing on the porch, sitting around. This baby gets off the bus and there's no quiet place for studying."

Neal said other students get home from school, have a nice meal, and then go to their rooms to study. But for many marginalized students, that is not an option.

"Kids don't have that," he said. "That teacher cried the whole way back. She said 'Mr. Neal, this baby's not going to have to worry about anything else. I understand what you're saying. I'm going to demand high expectations, but I can have some pencils and paper. I'm going to raise the bar.'"

Neal said many children in Nacogdoches come from single-parent homes in high poverty areas.

"You're not able to change that," he said. "But what you do, you do all you can for that child while he's there. I think it would be good to get in the community, to get to know the community and get to know the families."

During the time of integration, the schools and the military were the largest entities working toward bringing different races together. The problem, however, was that society was not always on board with these changes. So while African American students were attending school with White children, their African American parents were not welcome to work at White businesses. There was an unequal expectation for the future. Learning under the same roof as a child did not mean those children would be working under the same roof as adults. Having the opportunity to read out of new textbooks did not mean African American children would have the same opportunities in the real world.

"When we were separated, in a sense, a lot of us African Americans say we were stronger then," he said. "There were stronger ties in the community. We demanded performance, but as we came together, you lost a lot of that."

And those same divisions, he said, are alive and well today. Neal would like to see more businesses hire African American people for positions of authority. Children need to see that the sky really is the limit, he said. And with reports of police brutality and excessive force showing up in headlines across the nation on an almost weekly basis, Neal said more must be done to understand one another.

One of the things we've done in the school system throughout the years, we try to bring both communities together to have a sit down. Some of the superintendents over the past have done that, brought us together to the table to help us understand and build relationships. Those conversations aren't always easy, he said, but they must happen. "We're not where we need to be," he said. "We're going to continue to work and strive to get there, but we have to continue to build relationships and let the two communities come together."

Things have improved some, he said. There are more opportunities for people of Color. "I've had the opportunity myself," he said.

> "I've been very active in the community here, serving on the Chamber, becoming Chamber president. If the community had not opened up and come together, that would have never happened. I've served on different committees, and have been the chair of committees, and I realize we can do that. We try to model that for the young African American people. Prepare yourself, study, so when that time comes, you'll be available and be involved in the community. There are so many opportunities for our young people now."

Neal used to work in Human Resources for Nacogdoches ISD, and he actively recruited African American and Latin@/Hispanic American teachers, he said, because they were able to relate to the large population of Color that makes up the district. He would like to see banks and other businesses actively recruit people of Color, too.

"Can you imagine what this community would be like?" he said. "Let's just say in the banking business, we were not given an opportunity (before integration). And a lot of times it was not because of our ability, but it was because of the color of our skin. If you go downtown Nacogdoches, how many African American bankers are there? It's an area that hasn't really been penetrated, and it needs to be. It's going to take some aggressive recruitment and wanting them to be there."

What Nacogdoches needs, he said, are leaders.
"The community needs leadership that's going to pull us all together and open the doors and encourage the hiring of marginalized people," he said. "It's going to take communities growing together over the years. We've come a long way, in a sense, but we still have a long we to go. We have to be involved. We have to get out there."

References

Stephen F. Austin State University (N.D.) Community Collections Digital Archives Collections: E.J. Campbell School Yearbook. Retrieved from http://digital.sfasu.edu/cdm/compoundobject/collection/Community/id/415/rec/7

My Story: Experiencing the Racial Environment of the 60s and 70s in Nacogdoches, Texas

By: Verdis Daniels, Jr.

The trial of George Zimmerman put the conversation about race relations in the United States of America, in the national spotlight. Even President Barack Obama and Democratic State Representative from Minnesota Keith Ellison shared their experiences as young Black men and how Whites reacted to the color of their skin and not their actions. Writer Michael McAuliff of the Huffington Post (2014) wrote an article questioning whether attitudes toward race had improved since the Civil Rights Era. At the end of the article, McAuliff asked readers to submit stories on events in their lives where they encountered racial discrimination or profiling. As I thought about my life growing up in the East Texas town of Nacogdoches in the 60s and 70s, I could only recall one incident I personally encountered of racial profiling. But that one time was life altering. I often think about that night and wonder, why me? But I also give thanks to God, for only through his grace did the outcome end favorable to me.

Nacogdoches during that time was probably like most towns in the South. The early part of my life was in an environment of legalized segregation. There were separate facilities and institutions for Blacks and Whites. I attended all Black schools from the first through fourth grades. I lived in all Black neighborhoods and went to all Black churches. As a child, I hardly noticed. Even though the environment was segregated, it was an environment of strength, respect, and love. There was an emphasis on hard work and good behavior throughout the community. Academic achievement was highly valued. Parents expected their children to apply themselves in school. Meanwhile, they were fighting a battle to be accepted as equals and end the lawful separation and discrimination prevalent in the nation. I attended Emeline F. Carpenter Elementary School from the first through third grades and Brooks Quinn Jones in the fourth. The teachers were an extension of the community. High academic performance and good personal conduct were stressed. Parents relied on the teachers to reinforce the values taught at home. These teachers took pride in this charge for they were relatives, neighbors, and fellow church members. The Black teachers were highly respected and valued. They were civic leaders entrusted to mold the most valuable asset in the Black community, children, and prepare them to advance and take advantage of the opportunities the parents were fighting to obtain.

I had little contact with Whites. The neighborhood where I lived in 1968 was about one block from the all White high school, Nacogdoches High School. It was also close to downtown and bordered the White neighborhoods. We played sandlot baseball with some of the White kids, a couple were later classmates (Jim Horn and Sid Abernathy), and we got along well. Schools were still segregated, but there was a policy in place, Freedom of Choice, in which you could, chose the school you wanted to attend. Several kids in our neighborhood attended the White elementary school, Raguet.

As I entered the fifth grade I chose to attend Raguet School. There were two Black students in that fifth grade class, a girl from my neighborhood, Janice King, and me. During my time at Raguet, I did not experience any explicit racial incidents. I already knew Jim and Sid, and there were other kids I knew from Little League. The teachers were very supportive and pushed me academically, especially my homeroom teacher, Mrs. Muckleroy. One of my classmates, Randy Hull, and I became very good friends. Randy always included me in any activity that was going on. He probably assisted in my acceptance, not as a Black kid, but as a new kid. Randy got me involved in Boy Scouts, and that is the first time I became personally aware of the Black-White issue. My mother was very supportive of my attendance at Raguet. I know she had concerns because I was reminded to be on my best behavior and made to understand that I could not always do what my classmates did. However, I thrived socially and academically. I loved being in Boy Scouts and looked forward to my first camping trip. My mother said I could not go. She did not explain why, just that I couldn't go and it did not occur to me why. But as I look back I understand. She was being asked in 1969, to let her 10-year old son go camping in the woods for a weekend with White people she didn't know personally. This was at a time when I could not legally sit in a public place with the same kids. I give thanks to our Scout Leader and my step-father for convincing her to agree to allow me to go to the campout. I understand that it was one of the most nerve wracking times in her life. For me it was awesome. My squad leader was Cal Barton, an eighth grader. And as a Tenderfoot, my friends and I looked at squad leaders with admiration and respect. Cal personally watched out for me that weekend. While the other new guys were subjected to a Snipe Hunt, Cal made sure I was safe in camp. Cal made that first camping trip a memorable experience for the new guys in his squad. I still remember the tale of Indian Joe. and I am sure he opened our tent flap that night looking for a hand to replace the one he lost. Until he aged out of Boy Scouts, Cal made sure I was able to pass every test required to earn merit badges and move on to the next rank quickly. I count Cal as one of the people that had a positive influence on me.

In 1970 school segregation in Nacogdoches ended. I looked forward to my friends from Carpenter and Brooks Quinn meeting my friends from Raguet and getting a chance to share the experiences I had, but that was the innocence of youth. E. J. Campbell High School, the Black high school and Nacogdoches High School were combined. Nacogdoches High became the main campus. Black, gold, and white became the new school colors, which had been the colors of the White school, Nacogdoches High. E. J. Campbell ceased to exist. No more green and white. For older kids, integration exposed racial issues. Positions, offices, and titles that were important parts of high school were no more. Administrators decided since student body officers, club officers, and cheerleaders had already been decided for Nacogdoches High, E. J. Campbell students who were chosen for those positions would just lose out and have to wait for spring elections for the coming year. When elections came, not one Black student was elected to an office. The most visible discrepancy was for cheerleaders. There were no Black cheerleaders chosen.

The first year of integration, though full of challenges, showed promise. In time, politics destroyed that promise. In junior high, there were some challenges, but for the most part things were going well. There were fights, but these were more the result of changing hormones than racial animosity. However, we did follow the lead of older siblings, relatives, and neighbors and staged sit-ins and boycotts. The big event for the high schools was a walkout by the Black football players over the cheerleaders' election. A team that had advanced to bi-district in all team sports and had expectations of becoming a power based on the performance of the under classes was now in disarray. The impact affected Nacogdoches High for years to come.

Throughout high school, thanks to my counselor Mr. Purcell Warren, I was able to maintain a high level of academic performance. We battled over my course schedule. I wanted to be in classes with neighborhood friends. He kept putting me in advanced classes. Unlike most of the friends that I had attended Raguet with, I was not uncomfortable in these classes. I was more than capable of doing the work, but there was a social aspect missing. Even though I was good friends with the White students in class, there was no social interaction outside of school. Without Boy Scouts and sports, our communities were separated by historical barriers. Being in those classes made me a better student. I was pushed toward high academic achievement by those friends. They knew what I was capable of and expected me to excel. We were still friends, though that friendship did not extend beyond school and school activities. This environment led to me being selected to the National Honor Society, one of two Blacks selected. Pauletta Brown, a very good friend from school, was the the other. In my junior year I took the PSAT. Over the summer going into my senior year, I started receiving college catalogs. I had never really thought much about what school I would attend. Financially, college was out of the question, but I knew about the G. I. Bill and ROTC. As I was no longer playing sports, an athletic scholarship was not an option. I assumed all incoming seniors were receiving college material as every day more catalogs came with letters stating, "based on your outstanding academic achievement..." Some many catalogs came that the mailman would just give stacks to the people who worked in the office in the housing complex, Eastwood Terrace. Friends in the neighborhood would come and look at the catalogs. I became a celebrity of sorts.

When I started my senior year, my new counselor, Mrs. Frances Webster, met with me and started talking about college options. After months of looking and applying I finally landed a job at the Fredonia Hotel. My senior year was starting to look pretty good. It got better. The reason for all the college contacts became evident. I was recognized as a semi-finalist for the thirteenth annual National Achievement Scholarship program for Outstanding Negro Students, a program of the National Merit Scholarship Corporation. I was one of 1500 semi-finalists out of the 55,000 Black students that requested consideration when they took the 1975 Preliminary Scholastic Aptitude Test and National merit Scholarship Qualifying Test. A photographer from the Daily Sentinel came and took a picture of me with Mr. Warren and Mrs. Webster. The picture and article appeared in the paper. I was the pride of Eastwood Terrace. I was congratulated and recognized by all my classmates, schoolmates, the school faculty, and the community. My grandmother who always clipped out the honor roll list from the Daily Sentinel because I was on it was extremely proud. High academic performance, model citizen, hard worker, those words could be used to accurately describe me in 1976.

So as I pondered Mr. McAuliff's question and reflected on my life. I can say that despite growing up in Nacogdoches, Texas through segregation and integration, for 17 years and 10 months, I never personally experienced racial discrimination or profiling. But on November 6, 1976 that changed. On that night, in the eyes of two officers with the Nacogdoches Police Department, I was just a Black kid with no reason to be walking down Main Street at night. And to make matters worse, I had money in my pocket. Because of eight one dollar bills, in a matter of weeks, I went from being a news maker to a potential news item.

That Saturday morning, I woke up to the sound of a pounding rain. As I lay in bed, I thought about what I was going to do that day. The SAT was being administered in Lufkin, a town 20 miles south of Nacogdoches. I wasn't registered, but Mrs. Webster said I could go as a standby or wait for the next test. I was scheduled to work that day. Since I didn't know if I would be able to make it back on time, I chose to go to work. I had just started the job. Also Saturday was our busiest day with the popular buffet and I had no one to switch with. My mother came in and told me she was going to the washateria. She gave me eight dollars she had borrowed from me earlier in the week, eight one dollar bills. The rain had stopped. She asked if I needed a ride to work. I told her that was ok. I ended up catching a ride with my friend Bob on his brother's motorcycle. When I got to work, I was told the scheduled bus boy, John Wilson, was going to be late because he had a basketball game. So in addition to washing dishes, I had to bus tables and do room service until he came in. It continued to rain off and on throughout the day. It was a little after 10:30 p.m. when I clocked out. I was walking east down Main St. As I approached the intersection with Lanana St, I could see a police car parked on Lanana to my right. As I crossed Lanana, the police car accelerated and pulled in front of me in the drive of a service station on the corner. Two officers got out and approached me. The driver was of medium height. The passenger was tall and wore cowboy boots. The driver asked where I was going. I replied that I had just got off work and was heading home. The tall officer said: "you look just like that boy that robbed a lady earlier." I replied: "I have been at work at the Fredonia hotel since 2:00. You can go look at my time card." The tall officer said: "No! You are that boy that robbed the lady." He then started searching me. He found the eight one dollar bills in my pocket. He then said: "Yeah you the one." and grabbed his handcuffs. I kept insisting that I was at work, and they could go check my time card. I was told they didn't need to because they knew it was me. The driver then told me they needed to take me in to ask some questions. I said I would go, but they didn't have to handcuff me. I was placed in the back seat of the police car without cuffs.

When we got to the police station, the tall officer got out and opened my door. He then crouched in a linebacker stance and said "Boy don't you run." I had no intention of running. It looked kind of comical or should I say cliché`. I wanted to laugh, but I felt that would cause me a problem. The driver came around the car, looked at him and shook his head. He led me into the building. At that time I was not scared. I knew I had done nothing wrong. I was led into an interior room and told to sit down. Other officers started coming into the room. There was one Black officer that was known by my family, Officer Holman. He asked where I lived. I told him Eastwood Terrace. He then said "Oh you did it. I don't know what it is, but you are from the projects so you did it." I thought; wait until I tell my momma about this.

They stood me against the wall and took my picture with a Polaroid camera. I was told to sit down. While seated, the tall cop came toward me and stood on my toes. I told him that hurt and pushed him. As I pushed him I realized that was a mistake. He stepped back toward me, but at that time a Lieutenant came into the room. I recognized him from a summer program run by Officer Rice. They used to pick up kids and take us to play baseball or go swimming. I asked if he remembered me and told him what I was accused of. He looked around the room and said, "Let him go." I immediately left the building. I didn't think about retrieving my eight dollars the officers had taken when they first stopped me. As I walked toward the street. I saw a friend, Kendrick Deckard, who lived in Eastwood. He gave me a ride home. We talked about what had happened. It was a common thing to get stopped and taken in if you were out late at night. It had never happened to me, but other people I knew had experienced this. I thought nothing of it when I got home. I mentioned what happened to another friend, and we laughed about it. As I had done nothing wrong and was released, I did not mention the incident to my mother.

The following Monday when I got to work, I was told that the owner, Dan Stansil, needed to see me in his office to sign my W-4. When I got to his office. I saw Detective Jerry Weems sitting with him. I thought nothing of it as Det. Weems was a regular at the bar and restaurant. He often came into the kitchen and talked with the two elderly men, Mr. Flanagan and Mr. Brooks, who cleaned up at night. I tried not to talk to Det. Weems when he was there at night. He never showed them the respect I was taught to give elders. Both men were World War II vets, but he talked to them in a condescending way. Mr. Stansil told me that Det. Weems needed to talk to me. Det. Weems said the lady that was robbed identified me from the Polaroid as the person who robbed her, and I was being charged. I looked at Mr. Stansil and asked him to show my timecard as proof I was at work. He said there was nothing he could do, and I needed to go with the detective. I asked if I could call my mother and was told by Det. Weems I could do that from the station. As we were leaving, Mr. Stansil called my name and said: "I still need you to sign your W-4." I signed the W-4 and left with Det. Weems.

At the station I was taken into another room where I met with an officer. He started reading the charges against me; aggravated robbery and aggravated sexual assault. The officer wanted me to sign a confession and promised to drop the aggravated sexual assault if I signed. I told him I could not sign as I did not do what I was charged. The officer kept telling me I needed to sign, or I would go to trial on both charges. He kept stating that I needed to sign and mentioned my grandfather and mother. I said I could not admit to something I didn't do, and they would not want me to do so I told him my picture had been in the paper for outstanding academic achievement. Eventually he gave up. I can say that he was very professional and never tried to pressure me. He made no threats or effort to coerce me. Det. Weems came and took me to the county jail to be booked. At that that time, I asked if I could call my mother. He said I could make a call later. I was taken to a cell. I spent the night in jail. The next morning I waited to make my call home. Det. Weems never came. That afternoon I was told my mother had arrived. A guy that was a trustee recognized me and called to tell her I was in jail. I was taken downstairs and released to her custody. At that time Det. Weems asked if I still needed to make a call.

My mother told me that my uncle, William Sanders Jr,, had heard the police call on his scanner the day of the robbery. He knew that I did not fit the description. I had missed school Tuesday while I sat in jail. More importantly I had missed an assembly where the nominees for homecoming queen were to be presented. I was supposed to escort my half-sister Ethel Mae (Squeaky) Washington. She met me at my locker inquiring as to where I was in a not so kindly tone. I didn't tell her. But promised I would be at the game that Friday to escort her on the field. At least I was hoping to be there. I told no one at school what was going on. I felt embarrassed. I don't know why. That Friday I did make it to the game. Squeaky was 1st runner-up. Anne Jackson was 2nd runner-up. Within the school racial issues were not a problem.

My mother told me they had found a lawyer, Martha McCabe, and we were to meet with her. We met with Ms McCabe in her office. I did not know anything about her. Ms McCabe and her associates looked like university students in their jeans, loose shirts and casual shoes, much like I was dressed. Ms McCabe was passionate about her work.. Once she started talking about the case, my confidence in her abilities grew. I still was not confident in the Nacogdoches justice system. She was a woman, a Yankee, and she was defending a black kid. She took the clothes I was wearing the night I was stopped, and my statement as to what happened. She was aware of the police description; Black male around 6'2", brown pants, and blue jean jacket. I stood 5'8" and had on a maroon windbreaker and blue jeans. I also had on an oversized blue jean cap. Her fee was $600.00. I paid her with $200.00 form my savings, and my uncles paid the rest. I still think it ironic that the officers that stopped me that night felt I was guilty of something because I had eight dollars in my pocket. They didn't know I had a savings account at the Stone Fort National Bank, the premiere financial institution in town, with a balance over $200.00.

I had missed two days of work, Monday, the day I was charged, and Tuesday, the day I was released from jail. I was told I still had a job so I continued going to work. I was new, a dishwasher, and charged with committing a violent felony while on the clock. I worked at a hotel and had access to keys to every room in the hotel in addition to cash registers in the restaurant and bar. I was often the last employee, other than the cleaners, to leave the kitchen at night. A kitchen filled with meat, produce, and alcohol. Yet Mr. Stansil, Mr. Harrell, the co-owner, or none of the managers exhibited distrust in me. They offered neither support nor condemnation. They did not say anything to me about what happened. The lawyers came to the hotel and started questioning the staff that was at work that day. A couple of the waitresses expressed concern for me. They knew I was at work and could not understand how I could be charged. The owner made a comment to me one day that he wished my friends would stop coming to the hotel talking to the employees, referring to my lawyers. I told him they needed to get evidence to show I was innocent, and he could have helped at the beginning. He said nothing more to me. Det. Weems continued to visit the bar, and as was his habit, come through the kitchen. He did throw a couple of comments in my direction about my hippie lawyer.

One day Ms Mcabe's associate came and said the prosecutor had requested a hearing, and they needed me to be in court. He told me what they really wanted was to have me sitting in court so the victim could point me out. He, then, asked two of the waiters if they would go to court with me. We were all Black, but of varying heights and skin tones. The plan was to have us sit in different areas of the court. We were sitting outside the courthouse waiting. When the prosecutor realized what was happening the hearing was cancelled.

Before this incident, I was in the process of completing college applications with my counselor. Because of my situation, the application process was put on hold. I started looking into joining the military to take advantage of the GI Bill. I took the AFEES test and scored very high. The recruiter, TSgt. Reeves, told me based on my scores I could have qualified for an appointment to the Air Force Academy. But once again, because of my situation the Academy was not an option. If all was cleared, I could still join the Air Force, but the GI Bill eligibility was expiring on November 30, 1976. TSgt. Reeves kept in contact with Ms McCabe.

Ms McCabe contacted me and told me that the current DA, David Adams, was not seeking re-election. They had discussed my case with the new DA, Herb Hancock, and he could not figure out why I was charged. TSgt. Reeves called me and told me DA Hancock was going to drop the case once he got in office. Ms McCabe called me when the DA Hancock had formally dismissed the case. I met Ms McCabe in her office and retrieved my favorite jacket, the pants, and hat. For that aspect of my life, I was happy.

However, I had given up on college. Classmates were still congratulating me on being named a semi-finalist and inquiring about college choices. I told them I was undecided. I pretty much became withdrawn at school. None of my classmates were aware of what happened or if they were, no one approached me about it. I continued working at the Fredonia Hotel for a couple of weeks after the case was dropped. I couldn't figure why Mr. Stansil didn't stand up for me at the beginning. I had moved up to cook and filled in when the main cook was off. But I had bitterness toward Mr. Stansil and Det. Weems, who continued to come through as if nothing happened. I signed up for the delayed enlistment plan to join the Air Force. Finally, I just quit the hotel. After one month, I went back and got my old position as cook. I stayed at the hotel until graduation. During the final assembly, when academic awards were announced along with college acceptances, my name was not called. I'm sure people wondered why, but I didn't discuss what happened. I just told people I had enlisted in the Air Force.

The event of November 6, 1976 is something I think about daily. At first, it was easy to put aside, but as I got older, I thought about it more. I avoided class reunions. I made fewer visits to Nacogdoches. It was an issue I had to address when I joined the Air Force. It never came up again until I applied to the Internal Revenue Service. The arrest is on my record and shows up on any background checks. I did not' have to explain again for over 20 years. Not until I accepted a job with the Texas Workforce Commission. After 30 years, I still have to give an explanation. I started thinking about how despite all, things came out in my favor, such as the Lieutenant, that came in when I was being interviewed that Saturday night and Kendrick, driving by as I was leaving the police station. I would have had a long walk with an irate police officer to deal with. I was blessed with Ms. McCabe and her passion to fight for civil rights and fairness in the justice system and a DA that believed in justice over convictions produced a favorable outcome for me. There were teachers willing to speak on my behalf if the case went to trial. TSgt Reeves, who didn't need me to meet a recruitment quota, took personal interest in the outcome of the charges against me. But more than anything my family believed in me and the values they instilled throughout the ordeal. They stood behind me and provided the resources necessary in navigating the justice system.

I often think about how my classmates would take what happened to me. When you try to explain something like this to someone who was not involved it sounds hollow, even to me. I knew events like this happened. I didn't want people to pity me. Because I overcame this and put myself in a position to always have opportunities, I am not bitter and do not look at all Whites as supportive of racial discrimination. On the contrary, my life is an example of people showing respect for character. But there are people, flawed people that utilize policies, systems and institutions to do harm to others in a discriminatory way. I hope those that grew up with me see, through my story, that when people have discriminatory attitudes they can cause harm to innocents because they have not evolved in a changing world.

References

McAuliff, M. (2014, January, 23). Trayvon Martin and 2013 revealed harsh reality of racism in America. *The Huffington Post*. Retrieved from http://www.huffingtonpost.com/2014/01/01/2013-racism_n_4525622.html.

I Have a Voice, So Listen!

By: Brooke Taylor-Johnson, Dr. Brandon L. Fox, and Dr. Patrick S. De Walt

I, Brooke Taylor-Johnson, was once told that the most powerful weapon I have is my story. My mentor told me that *it* was within me, but that I just have not realized *it* yet. I have been blindly searching for this *thing* that was going to help me do what I was put on this earth to do. I was searching so relentlessly that I missed this *thing* that has been with me my entire existence: my personal experiences and circumstances. *I have a voice; I am the story.*

Athough I come from a loving home and a family that wishes nothing but the best for me, growing up was not the easiest. I come from a working class background with an absent father who I was lucky to visit with once a year and a single mother working a hourly-waged job while also struggling to raise her three daughters. As a child, I was sickly and did not utter a sound until the age of five years old. My speech pathologist at the time wrote in her notes (which I still have to this very day) that I would most likely be placed in special education classrooms my entire educational career. Due to my condition, my eldest sister would often miss out on going to school herself to stay at home with me during her high school years.

Over time, my eldest sister found herself engaged in various types of trouble. She was in and out of motel rooms, Women's Shelters, and often found herself homeless. My middle sister was also in and out of trouble and often found herself in the hospital due to her troubles. My mom could not leave her job, so by the time I was a teenager I was taking care of my sister's six children while going to school and maintaining my grades. Although I cared for my sisters' children to the best of my ability, I was unable to protect them from their daily realities which included domestic violence, homelessness, controlled substances, servere health problems, and lack of food. This is what these children endure on a regular basis. The experiences that my sisters' children have endured through their short existences are similar to what countless marginalized children in rural East Texas experience in their everyday life (Delpit, 2006, 2013). Many will explain that it is the norm for them. Being a student in a rural East Texas school district throughout my primary and secondary education, I witnessed numerous instances where students lived in certain conditions that were both unhealthy and dangerous, such as children who went home to an empty house with no one to feed them, no one to assist them with their homework, or no one to simply talk to them about their day at school. Unfortunately, I have also witnessed educators who seem to have inadequate training, dispositions, and/or experience with children from challenging socioeconomic backgrounds and a lack of knowledge about the realities of the children of Color in rural East Texas.

The motivation for this chapter is simple: to impact construction of an environment that responds to the realities of the African American children of Nacogdoches. It is with hope that the voices from this chapter will positively impact the consciousness of classroom teachers, school administrators, school board officials, and the community of Nacogdoches as a whole. As authors, we believe that one way to eradicate oppressive borders is through paying special attention to the voices and stories from those who have--and in many ways continue to--experience marginalization. Furthermore, these experiences represent both individual and collectivized stories that often are not afforded the time or space to be represented. Within the following sections, these important voices are expressed to not only be seen but also heard.

Expression: Voice and Storytelling

Centralizing narratives, storytelling, and other voice-focused outlets can draw attention to specific realities that we live each day. Critical race theorists utilize voice "as a way to illustrate and underscore broad legal principles regarding race" (Ladson-Billings, 2013, p. 42). Within critical race theory (CRT), we have to be conscientious and must value expression while also recognizing the environment in which realities occur. The realities that students of Color face in rural East Texas often include struggles with structural poverty through racialized capitalism (Leong, 2013; Stovall, 2013), historically induced power structures (Bell, 2005), and negative perceptions of character and intelligence (Hayman, 2000; Steele, 2009).

In this chapter, we take two unique approaches to magnify expressed voice. The first is through direct, independent storytelling. During the initial research process, we were notified by a former student in rural East Texas asking us to share her story. The second approach to draw attention to experience was through conversations within the community. A community member assisted us in identifying eight former students who each attended the same local, rural, public East Texas ISD within the past five years. The focus of each conversation within the community was to discuss their experiences as a student in a rural East Texas ISD. Each participant identified as African American, Black, Black American, or a person of African descent. Five participants identified as female and three participants identified as male. In sharing their stories, we attempt to present their experiences through the application of authentic voice and representation.

Independent Storytelling: Seen, but NOT Heard

I, Brittany Thomas, first realized *it* after switching from a school attended predominantly by students of Color over to a school that was predominately White in third grade. The first day of school, after going over basic rules and regulations, our teacher sat us on the rug for story time. I was lucky to have my best friend in class with me, so I sat by her. While the teacher was reading, two White girls--also best friends--were carrying on about something extra, and we couldn't hear the story. I leaned over and said, "If you don't shut up so we can hear the story I'm going tell the teacher." The classroom phone rings and the teacher walks near the door, answers, and steps out into the hall for about five minutes. When she entered the room, the girl I'd whispered to and her best friend jumped up and yelled, "Mrs! Mrs!" With tears flooding down their faces said, "Brittany and Ashley said if we didn't stop talking they would kill us!" I was sitting with a puzzled look on my face because I said no such thing. Ashley and I, along with others surrounding us, tried to explain the teacher, but the White female teacher refused to hear it. She told us to get our things, she called our parents, and she escorted us to the office.

Our teacher didn't want to hear our side of the story because "we *looked* like we said it." How do two innocent third grade girls that have never been in trouble inside or out of the school *look* like they'd threaten to kill somebody? At this point, we were both faithful church goers and members of many church organizations. We did not look like we'd threaten them. We looked Black versus the fact that they were White. The worst part is, the principal, also a White female, didn't even ask us what happened. She automatically went along with the story she was given and suspended Ashley and me for three days.

This was my first time ever getting in trouble at school. This somehow led to a spiral of trouble for me. I vowed that day that I'd seek revenge on all three of those White women, the teacher, and those two little girls. My best friend, on the other hand, was extremely kind, fragile, and very sensitive. She was devastated when we were suspended. Her grandparents were so mad. Days later, the girls confessed to having lied on the first day which for some reason did not excuse our absences from being suspended, did not remove the write up in our school file, did not dry the tears that Ashley had cried, did not calm the anger that rose inside of me, did not make up the time we'd missed bonding with our classmates, did not catch us up on the lessons they'd taught, and did not make me look at them or those faculty members any different. The worse part of it all was the fact that they weren't even punished. The teacher's exact words to my momma were, "Awww, they're just kids being kids. You know, they say kids say the darnedest things." They got away with lying and saying we threatened them with murder because they were White in a predominantly White school. *I have a voice, I am the story. This was my reality.*

Analysis. Within oppressive educational contexts, hegemony and racism often occupy critical aspects of the learning environment. Perceptions of those who are often viewed as "the Other" are situated in a level of hypersensitivity in which they did not create. Yet, they are perceived guilty without an opportunity for due process. In many ways, Ashley and Brittany were guilty by perception due to their race and body as mechanisms for student accountability and discipline. They were being subjected to an objective examination as "racialized other." As Fanon (2008) illuminates within his concept of third person consciousness, "I was responsible not only for my body but also for my race and my ancestors" (p. 92). This imposed responsibility continues the historical disconnect between aspects of justice and "Black" bodies within the United States and as well as its school systems (Chapman, 2013; Delpit, 2006; Du Bois, 2003; Fanon, 2008).

Conversation One: Perceptions with Power

Crystal: When I was in high school, I feel like I had mostly positive experiences. I didn't get in trouble, I was friends with everybody, I wasn't placed in in-school-suspension (ISS), and I made good grades. However, as I reflect back now, a lot happened under my nose that I did not know about.

Terrence: I remember during my freshman year of high school going to this lady trying to get help and she coming to me like I had a sob story. She asked: "Is there something wrong?" and I replied, "No, I just need to finish this thing. I need help with number three." Then this guy behind me, that doesn't look like me came in, and she sat him down pulled out his books for him and helped him but left me in the corner because she thought something was wrong with me.

Crystal: So because you're Black, you think she felt that something was wrong with you, or that you don't have a father figure at home?

Terrence: Right! I have both my parents at my house, just in case you didn't know. I'm good. I needed help on number three. I am telling you. I remember that number. I needed help on number three. Right. This is not only from me that you will hear this from. This is from every Black student, because she just feels like we go through… [Monica interjects]

Monica: There was this Principal. I had a teacher who was telling me that our Principal used to call the Hispanic and the Black people "The Other Kids." Like yeah! He would say the White kids and "The Other Kids." And he used to always talk about "The Other Kids" in like the meetings. He would be like, "Our 'Other Kids' aren't meeting the standards of the White kids." And I was like "really!"

Crystal: He actually encouraged me to go to Pre-AP. I mean he was so adamant about me going to Pre-AP. He was on me every single day. He would say, "Please go to Pre-AP." I would have never thought he would say something like that.

Monica: I was in my Pre-AP classes, because I take all advanced classes cause, you know, my parents were like, "Well, you're smart enough for it, go for it." I've been the only Black child in all of my Pre-AP classes and, you know, like the teachers always look at me like, "Why are you in here?" Just because I am Black doesn't mean that I don't know everything these White kids know. Like, why, why single people out? Like, we are all the same. The skin shouldn't matter. I feel, as long as you're getting an education, it shouldn't matter what our color is or, you know, like as long as we are making good grades then they shouldn't worry about oh, the other group isn't working as hard as the White people, because the White kids aren't smart either.

Yolanda: I remember during my freshman year, I didn't have a lot of diversity in my AP class. They felt like Black students couldn't do it, like we had a lack of intelligence or that we weren't able to comprehend what someone was saying, and I did feel like that wasn't right. Because me being in the class means that I am capable of the intelligence that White people have, and I know what I am doing, but I don't need anyone to remind me. So, it was like going into the classroom was a negative vibe. So you would sit there and try to get help, but then they felt like because you needed help and because you didn't understand it that you didn't belong there.

I wanted to understand it and understand it to the fullest potential that I could so I know what I am doing. I didn't feel like the opportunity was open for me because I was Black, but if a White student had a question, and it was answered in any way that you wanted it, the teacher would even come over and help you do it and I feel like that opportunity should have been offered to me as well. I know one time I was in AP World Geography and there were two Black students. There was me and a friend of mine. I had a question about trying to figure out how I was supposed to do a project, and I didn't understand because I hadn't been there the day before because I had to attend a track meet.

When I got there the next day, I started asking questions about the project, and she felt like I should have just known what to do because I was in the AP class. I noticed later that another student had a question, and she answered it. She gave her the full layout. She gave her the slides from the presentation and everything. When I asked her for help again, she told me that I should have known what I was doing. If I couldn't understand it and pick up on it, then I didn't deserve to be there in the first place.

Crystal: Oh, wow!

Terrence: No, she didn't! I went through that in my junior year in my Physics class. In my Physics class, he didn't always necessarily look over the Black people, but he will help the top person that knows he got it in class, but if we got a question, he will tell us to hold up and never come back. Why would you help your number one student more than your lower students? The number one student in class is White. His average is a one hundred through, and he can't help these people who are making 40s and 50s in the class?

Karen: A one hundo?!

Terrence: And he is saying that it is their fault when they call and ask for help and you put them on hold and never come back.

Yolanda: One positive experience that I've had is that a few of the teachers do see that you have the potential to do things later on. So, they try and help you, but other than that if they don't really see something in you or find that you are worth their time then they won't try and offer you any help.

Karen: I remember when I first came here there wasn't a lot of teachers that saw potential, but there was this one principal, and she always told me to do this and do that, and when I got in middle school she moved up to middle school with us. and she always encouraged me, and she wasn't my color. If there was ever a time that I needed help, she always came to help me every time. So, like, if I ever needed a notebook, she gave me that. If I ever needed anything, she was always there and wasn't like a sympathy thing. She just did it out the kindness of her heart.

Sage: Dang! Why are y'all looking at me?

Terrence: Experiences?

Sage: Well, I had one. An English teacher told me that I needed five more years of school when I graduated high school, because I didn't answer one question.

David: My freshman year I was in Geometry, and I was the only Black guy in there because this was the year they had started the "if you wanna get ahead take Algebra I in 8th grade." So, I did that, and I was the only Black that was in Geometry. So, they would always throw out the Black jokes, and the little White girls would always throw out the Black jokes. There were two Hispanics in there. One of them, he took offense to, he was taking offense to what they were doing making jokes at me. So I guess he snitched to the principal or somebody. So they called everybody, all the White girls, all the White boys, in, and they were all like "What's going on? What's with all the Black jokes?" You know? So, I was just like, "You know, I don't really care. I am making good grades in there that's all I'm in there for anyway." So when we went back to class later that day they were all just like, "See, that's exactly what you expect to do when you don't have your little Black friends with you, so you go and snitch on us." And I was like, "That's not what I did. I was big chillin." And then when a Black person makes a good grade on a test… [Monica interjects]

Monica: They get mad. They get upset.

David: First it's, "Oh, David made a good grade!" Well, the White person made a good grade, too. You didn't explode about them. You didn't give them balloons and flowers.

Monica: And then, I hate when the teacher like, they'll put "awesome" on the White kids paper if they make a one hundred or whatever, but when it comes to the Black kids, and they have a one hundred, oh it's just a hundred.

David: And if you compare the papers, sometimes you will have the same answer, and you just be like, "We have the same answer. How did I get this wrong and you got it right?" But you really got it right.

Monica: Oh, I'm sorry. Let me go change that.

David: I always hate the White teachers that always do that. I compare my tests and assignments with the White girls. I know that if they got it right sometimes we both would have the right answer, but mine has an "x," or we both have it wrong, but they have it right. You know? I have this White friend. The first time I met her, I was being stereotypical. I felt like she was one of those White girls that wouldn't want to talk to me because of the color of my skin. And she said, "Hello" and, you know? I guess she saw that I wasn't a dog. I guess as we got closer she told me, "I thought you would be like the others." Like, I understood what she was talking about, but still she was like, "I thought you would be like the other Black guys. You didn't look like it." She was like, "You didn't curse and try to get at me like the Black guys. You weren't like that." She said, "That's why I can't really talk to Black guys." I told her, "Well, you have to know people first."

Monica: Not all Black people are the same.

David: And even if they are, they're all still people.

Terrence: For the simple fact of the reputation of our school district even before me, I always try to have at least one Black teacher on my schedule just to know that I will have somebody that will push me to do better. Like, it was always cool for me to see. It's cool to have a White teacher, but it's different when you have a Black teacher telling you that you can do this, because she's already been there, and she already been through this. OK, you're my inspiration. I can do exactly what you are doing.

Crystal: So, do you think that it benefits you to see people of Color in high places like the president or a teacher in the classroom?

Terrence: Right. It does help. When you do that, your grade will go up in that class more than any other class because you feel like she is going to push you to do better.

Crystal: Like she understands you?

Terrence: Right, she understands me. Even when I thought I was going to fail, this teacher was not racist herself. She helped the White people just as much as she helped the Black people.

Analysis. Through the process of dialogue, many shared themes surfaced. The student-to-teacher and student-to-student interactions clearly influenced not only how the students saw themselves, but also how they saw themselves perceived. In doing so, they further embody what Fanon's concept *third person consciousness* sought to explore. These perceptions often contained a level of pathology. As demonstrated within Terrence's story, "she [the teacher] thought something was wrong with me" suggests how perceptions of race and the body constitute the teaching and learning environments for students of Color. It also suggests that the words of W. E. B. Du Bois (2003) still hold validity in the current lived experiences of African American/Black students, "How does it feel to be a problem?" (p. 8).

These interactions have significant impacts on student identity. Cross (1991), within his discussion on *nigrescence*, presents notions of "spotlight, or race image, anxiety" offers a lens to understand aspects of the stories presented. Being the only student of Color in a class or having to offset preconceived notions about membership within a racialized cultural group often places students of Color in precarious position within their educational and social environments. This statement by Monica captures key elements of Cross's analysis: "I've been the only Black child in all of my Pre-AP classes and, you know, like the teachers always look at me like, 'Why are you in here?'"

Conversation Two: Dress

David: They are trying to make sure they find somebody with the littlest thing to get them in trouble.

Monica: Yeah, me being in the hallways and stuff, I'm not a troublemaker. I'm not the type of student that gets in trouble at all, but like some of the teachers like, you can tell when they have their favorites or when they're picking at people. Principal Jones, she talked about how we can't wear all these different clothes or types of material. She has to realize that some of us are born with these traits or you know or like it runs in our family. She picks her favorites too. With the tights and the long shirts, she allows the White girls to wear it, but when it comes to the girls of Color, she has a problem with it, and she'll make us change clothes or have us sent home, or she might even give us D-Hall or send us to ISS and with the guys they come with those new joggers or whatever?

David: They're tight around the ankles.

Samuel: Also, during my junior year I was walking down to my football period, and it was a Black boy and a White boy walking down, side-by-side, pants you know the same length. They were saggin', I mean, both of them was [*sic*]. They were walking together. Well, Mrs. Jones stopped the Black dude. "You need to pull up your pants. We don't do that here at school." Looks right at the White boy "Hey, how are you?" and lets him keep going. That really just rubbed me the wrong way, like, you're going to stop this dude about his pants and the White dude is the same way…OK, why?

Monica: Yeah, some White guys will be wearing something, and she won't say anything to them, but when a male of Color walks by her and has them on she has a problem with it. And then the whole thing with the earrings! I [have] seen a White guy, walk past the principal with earrings in his ear and she said not a thing to him, but when it came to Erik Johnson… do y'all know him?

Crystal, David, and *Samuel*: No…

Monica: Oh, when it came to him and he had his earrings in his ear they made him call his mom, and this is before his mom started working in the district, but they made him call her to come up there just to get him for having earrings in his ear.

Crystal: Such a waste of time and energy for him being a student up there. He could be learning instead [of] going home to change a pair of earrings. Take them out and take them out of the other child's ear too.

Monica: Exactly! And that's the thing. That's what I don't get about them… [David interjects]

David: I mean is it a distraction at all?

NACOGDOCHES: Integration and Segregation, Then and Now

Monica: I don't feel that it is a distraction as long as you're up there learning.

David: It's not a distraction. You're saying, "You cannot wear this!" So when one person does wear it, it's a distraction and everybody pouncing.

Samuel: I feel like if they were more concerned about our education than what we wear, our school would be a lot better that what it is now.

Monica: Yes, a whole lot better.

Crystal: When I was up there, it was "Tuck in your shirt. Tuck in your shirt." That's all I ever heard. "Why are you wearing flip-flops? You can't wear flip-flops." I am trying to think if it was my senior year or junior year when they finally got rid of the tucking in of shirts. I believe they saw that we were still going to untuck our shirts. We're not going to tuck them in. They noticed that they were saying that more often than "How are you today? How was your day? How are your grades?"

David: That's the first thing on their mind. "Oh, let me see what he has on. Let me make sure he doesn't have on any... Let me see if his pants are up."

Crystal: What gets me is when you look at a child's waist line first instead of looking at that child in their eyes first and beginning a conversation in a respectful by saying, "Hello, how are you?" That's a human being. That child is not an item. You don't need to look at me like that. Don't look at my waist line first then look at me in my face. Look me in my face and be respectful to me and then you can see whether I am in dress code. I remember one time when I was wearing a t-shirt and if had a giraffe on it, no. I am sorry; it had a dinosaur on it. It was like a little green dinosaur, cartoon looking dinosaur. It had a chain with a "D" for dinosaur. It had some type of saying on it. It was nothing bad or anything like that, no gun violence, none of that. No gang violence, nothing, it was silly, basically a kid shirt. The principal looked at me and as she walked up to me, she kind of tilted her head said, "Oh," and then walked away because she saw that there was nothing wrong with my shirt. How do you get something bad from a green dinosaur wearing a chain with a "D" and some small writing on the side? She just knew she was going to get me. That's what she did.

Samuel: Like I said earlier, I totally understand that the district wants to be "top notch" and wants their students to look the part... [Monica interjects]

Monica: I'm sorry, but we will never get there as long as they keep setting these rules to specific colors and race. We will never be that type of "top notch" district. No.

Samuel: I understand and they want to be that part, you know? They won't fit in and everything, but I mean, I know some friends, just to throw this out there, I know some friends that's in San Antonio right now going to school, and they are not down there telling them what they can wear or whatever. I compare their school to our school, and I totally see the difference in education down there than we do up here. I mean, if honestly you put all your effort into our grades and our education and what we are learning instead of what we have on or what we look like. I mean, you could have the most beat down people at your school, but they can be smart. They may look beat down to you or whatever, but when someone comes up and acknowledges them, talk to them and they give this answer that you wouldn't expect that's way more than what you look like. It's one thing to look the part, but you have to have, you know, the education to be the part. So, that's how I feel about the dress thing. Don't worry too much about what we dress like or what we look like. When somebody comes up "Hey! How are you doing? Oh, I'm doing fantastic! How are you?" You're like, Whoa! This person is not how I thought he was. That's what makes Nacogdoches and their school the part.

Analysis. The shared student experiences here contextualize an environment in which students' bodies are a canvas for interpretation. From the perspectives of our participants, those *somebodies* are often encapsulated in Black and Brown skins. Yet, these interpretations form a false binary that ultimately places students in compromised positions between being themselves and being what the school policy requires. David also spoke to this when he stated, "They are trying to make sure they find somebody with the littlest thing to get them in trouble." Crystal expressed some level of frustration to this positioning when she stated "What gets me is when you look at a child's waist line first instead of looking at that child in their eyes first. Look me in my face and be respectful to me, and then you can see whether I am in dress code."

Through several of these different accounts, our participants have shared their perspectives on how they saw education as secondary to the negatively held perceptions regarding what they wore and how they looked. Samuel's statement clearly captures this sentiment, "I feel like if they were more concerned about our education than what we wear, our school would be a lot better that what it is now." Yet, this perspective is not free from opposition as he goes on to state, "Like I said earlier, I totally understand that the district wants to be 'top notch' and wants their students to look the part…" However, looking the part first requires those who are professionally obligated to acknowledge, value, and respect the historical legacies and cultural representations embodied within their students and families. As Crystal poignantly states, "looking at that child in their eyes first and beginning a conversation in a respectful [way] by saying, 'Hello, how are you?' That is a human being. That child is not an item. [That child has a voice; that child has a history.]"

Discussion

In bringing our participants' stories to the center, many aspects of their backgrounds connect with overarching themes within the discourse on educational experiences of students of Color. No matter how often their stories are explored, aspects remain that present structural, educational, and social barriers to their growth and advancement. Within the following sections, further exploration of themes derived from participants' shared narratives are highlighted. In particular, notions of educational minefields and a surveilled present as it defines and/or denies access to their histories.

Educational Minefields:
Negotiating Self, Environment, and Learning

Historically, the pursuit of education and learning have been tied to negotiations of identity and the navigation of varied social environments (Anderson, 1988; Du Bois, 1979; Lemert & Bhan, 1998; Morgan, 1995; Woodson, 2006). Through each instance, this pursuit placed persons of African descent in figurative minefields. Minefields constructed through social, political, and legal actions have created challenges to societal struggles that denied people of Color their humanity and access to opportunity (Appiah & Gates, Jr., 2004). The stories captured within this chapter continue to illuminate the multiple minefields that many schools represent for African American/Black learners. Those minefields include school disciplinary actions, challenges when it comes to being and expressing 'giftedness,' being bound by gendered historical norms, the stigmatization of youth due to perceptions of social and cultural capital, and, equally important, the results of living and learning in increasingly racialized educational and social environments (Bonner, II, 2014; Perry, Steele, & Hilliard, 2003). Yet, these obstacles are cloaked within a system that steadily replaces students' humanity with statistical data justifying educational and social policies that further support a hegemonically racialized society that averts addressing its problems. Students of Color, when positioned for disciplinary actions, are often labeled as "problems" first. Disciplinary data continue to provide evidence of racially disproportionate actions (see Table 1).

Table 1
Specific Rural East Texas ISD for Academic Year 2014-2015 (TEA, 2015)

Race/Ethnicity	Number of Students in the specific Rural East Texas ISD	Percent of students in the specific Rural East Texas ISD	DAEP Placements	Out of school suspensions	In school Suspensions
African American/Black	1,857	28.9%	55	748	1,728
Latino/Latina/Hispanic American	2,890	45.0%	29	305	1,067
European American/White	1,391	21.7%	< 5	108	391

The voices presented in this chapter add context to the data regarding the disproportionality between student groups as it relates to disciplinary actions by the district. The largest student population groups are represented by their overall percentage of the total student population -- 1,857 (28.9%) African American/Black, 2,890 (45.0%) Latino/Latina/Hispanic American, and 1,391 (21.7%) European American/White. These numbers illustrate a huge disparity in terms of who is disciplined and who is not. As Brittany's story emphasizes, there was a significant difference in disciplinary actions regarding suspensions administered to African American/Black students and European American/White students. The data addressing

"In School Suspensions" captures this disparity between these two student groups: 1,337 instances. The data for "Out of School Suspensions" is not any better: 640 instances.

Texas school disciplinary data has come under fire since the Breaking Schools' Rules report by the Council of State Governments and the Public Policy Research Institute (Fabelo et al., 2011). The study highlighted that 97% of all suspensions and expulsions were for a violation of school codes as deemed by campus teachers and administrators (Fuentes, 2014). Only 3% of suspensions and expulsions were for offenses that required mandatory disciplinary punishment. Similar to the data provided for this specific rural East Texas ISD, African American/Black students were disproportionately punished when compared to European American/White students.

The student code of conduct states that there are nine types of general conduct violations: disregard for authority, mistreatment for others, property offenses, possession of prohibited items, possession of telecommunications or other electronic devices, possession of drugs, misuse of technology resources and the internet, safety transgressions, and miscellaneous offenses. The voices presented above shared a consistent concern about dress and appearance. While negotiating perspectives of racialized femininity and masculinity, students must also adhere to a racialized dress code. Under miscellaneous offenses, students shall not violate dress and grooming standards as communicated in the student handbook. According to the student handbook, "the district's dress code is established to teach grooming and hygiene, prevent disruption, and minimize safety hazards. Proper dress is extremely important for school morale and safety. We at ---- Middle/High School adhere to a *conservative dress* [emphasis added] for all students. A properly dressed student affords better behavior and improved school climate."

What does conservative dress consist of? At first glance, the guidelines suggest that conservative dress is historically connected to Whiteness (and we should state our assumption that Christianity is directly associated with Whiteness). It is interesting to see a direct focus of district guidelines to counter popular dress and grooming trends that have become a cultural staple in *some* communities of Color. District guidelines directly target body piercings (females) chains, grilles, earrings (for males), hoodies, headwear, sagging, and sunglasses. The district guidelines also emphasize female modesty that reinforces historical notions of White female bodies as "pure" juxtaposed to the historical notions of the oversexualization of Black female bodies. Although the policy is apparent to all students, regardless of race, Whiteness directly influences the construction and application of district policy. Furthermore, Whiteness also impacts the way that dress and appearance are surveilled.

Voices presented in this chapter provide evidence of the over-surveillance of students of Color (Chapman, 2013). For example, David stated that "They are trying to make sure they find somebody [referring to students of Color] with the littlest thing to get them in trouble." Monica followed, "With the tights and the long shirts, she allows the White girls to wear it, but when it comes to the girls of Color, she has a problem with it, and she'll make us change clothes or have us sent home or she might even give us D-Hall or send us to ISS…" School personnel are more focused on the behavior and dress of students of Color, therefore increasing the likelihood that they face disciplinary measures -- disciplinary measures that negatively impact educational access, intellectual growth, and educational success (Chapman, 2013).

A Surveilled Present: Denying History through Miseducation, Symbolic Racism, and Social Dogma

Within CRT discourse, the problematization of the educational experiences of students of Color is further impacted by the practice of surveillance (Chapman, 2013). This process of being surveilled is represented through the realities of people of African descent within the United States during the antebellum and postbellum periods continuing through the modern moment. Yet, as Du Bois (1979) stated, the Veil still remains and continues to be a haunting historical reminder of how students of Color are seen, taught, and ultimately punished within environment of learning. De Walt (2009) discusses Du Bois's concept:

> This "Veil" held various forms that included "Race" and "Color" within Du Bois's text. In understanding "the Veil" one has to understand how it co-exists with the "color-line." In a sense, the lifting of "the Veil" through the awakening of "double consciousness" allows one to see the problem of the twentieth century as the "color-line." (p. 67)

In many instances, the narratives of our participants identify how "the Veil" is and has been enacted within their learning experiences. Whether "the Veil" takes the form of stereotypical perspective of their family structure, intellectual abilities, and/or the physical presence within these spaces, the levels of students' consciousnesses are being heightened. Through recognition of "the Veil," the following aspects of their experiences must also take center stage: miseducation, symbolic racism, and social dogma.

Miseducation. Carter G. Woodson's (2006) analysis of miseducation of people of African descent is an important component of this chapter:

> The opponents of freedom and social justice decided to work out a program which would enslave the Negroes' mind inasmuch as the freedom of body had to be conceded. It was well understood that if by the teaching of history the [W]hite man could be further assured of his superiority and the Negro could be made to feel that he had always been a failure and that the subjection of his will to some other race is necessary....If you can control a man's thinking you do not have to worry about his actions. (p. 84)

In engaging the participants' stories, it was clear that the participants did not feel as though they were being educated with their cultural heritages in mind through the practices of culturally responsive pedagogy and/or culturally responsive teaching (Gay, 2010; Sleeter & Cornbleth, 2011). Access to learning about Black history was rare, as depicted by the collection of narratives below. These selections represent a snapshot of their resurfacing thoughts pertaining to learning about Black history. As a result, we recognized a need to highlight them as the participants acknowledge the importance of history while also indicating the lack of access both through school activities and personal interactions.

Karen: My English teacher, he did a little bit about it, but for me, Mr. Jameson, he is a White person, and he helps me a lot.

Terrence: I can say this about Mr. Jameson. The only thing he did for me was…what he did for me…we had Black poems and I picked "Let America be America Again" and all of them. So, that was in February, and I appreciate that. For Black History, that's all you got if you didn't have his class. Nothing was spoken about Langston Hughes, Dr. Martin Luther King, Malcom X, Rosa Parks. Nothing was spoken about anybody that even walked. Posters weren't put up. If you were not in Student Council, you would know nothing about that. It was just terrible. Now we did have a Black History Program, which was okay. It was good, but at the same time, you didn't know anything if you didn't do anything. So therefore, we don't know where we came from and we keep letting history repeat, just like it is now.

Crystal: It hurts to know that Black history was not talked about like it should be. The only thing that I can remember really is the Black history program that the Students' of Color organization puts on every year.

Access to a representative history is an important component of a healthy self-identity (Cross, 1991; Woodson, 2006). These shared stories highlight the need for positive and relevant role models and historical figures for students of Color. This call is not solely for schools and districts to check off that a diversity requirement or initiative was met on their administrative reports. Moreover, this call is fundamentally needed to provide meaningful connections with the curriculum and the child. Pedagogically, doing so affords a better learning experience and opportunity for all parties involved including the teacher.

Symbolic Racism. Jones (1997) identifies the work of Sears (1988) in explaining what many of our participants encountered within their learning experiences as *symbolic racism*. According to Jones (1997), "*symbolic racism* was defined as the intersection of antiblack sentiment and feeling and a strong endorsement of the traditional U.S. values of individualism reflected in the Protestant work ethic" (p. 124). Within our participants' shared stories, themes that are often associated with "traditional U.S. values" as well as those associated with being a "model student" continued to surface. It is unclear whether this notion of "traditional U.S. values" meant coming from a two-parent home as Terrence stated, "I have both [of] my parents at my house" or as Brittany shared, "we were both faithful church goers and members of many church organizations."

Terrence and Brittany's lived experiences are situated within these normative values and expectations and through these experiences, it is obvious to them that they have experienced an educational context that conveys anti-Black sentiment. For Terrence, it was the stigmatization of Black families as being incomplete or dysfunctional, and for Brittany, this sentiment manifested itself in false accusations of violence that although refuted, never was afforded exoneration. Others' stories like David's experience with "the Black jokes" align themselves with the concept of racial microagressions (Huber & Solorzano, 2015; Profit, Mino, & Pierce, 2000; Solorzano, 1998).

Huber and Solorzano (2015) articulate racial microaggressions as "a form of systematic, everyday racism used to keep those at the racial margins in their place" (p. 302). David's narrative provides a clear example of this as his story unfolded where White students, after being questioned by the principal, stated "See, that's exactly what you expect to do when you don't have your little Black friends with you, so you go and snitch on us." While David expresses within his narrative that "That's not what I did. I was big chillin." His statements do not necessarily mask the potency of racial microagressions as a result of this experience. Huber and Solorzano (2015) provide three important forms of racial microagressions:

1. verbal and non-verbal assaults directed toward People of Color, often carried out in subtle, automatic or unconscious forms;

2. layered assaults, based on race and its intersections with gender, class, sexuality, language, immigration status, phenotype, accent, or surname; and

3. cumulative assaults that take a psychological, physiological, and academic toll on People of Color. (p. 302)

David's experience, as with many of the other participants, can be linked to these three articulated forms as students within the district and school.

When using racial microaggresssions in concert with symbolic racism, the harsh effects of the educational space can be seen as a toxic environment. It becomes more difficult to discern these racialized attacks from the cloak of traditional values and school policies when they are positioned as the cultural and social norms. Often when students of Color are confronted, such as when Brittany and Ashley were falsely accused of making a violent threat, the concerns of students of Color are dismissed through statements embodied here, "Awww, they're just kids being kids. You know, they say kids say the darnedest things."

Social Dogma. The concept of social dogma is an important aspect of our participants' experiences that needs to be addressed. This concept requires a person "to accept beliefs without questioning them" (Koppelman & Goodhart, 2011, p. 6). Having this understanding is even more important when considering the context in which our participants are learning and growing in rural East Texas. From a sociocultural perspective, there remain fundamental tenets that govern many of the family and social structures within this region. These tenets include but are not limited to religion, class, language, and race/ethnicity/culture.

What further complicates this milieu is that most are embedded as social constructs that socialize communities to conform and not reject and/or question. This is at the heart of not only social dogma but the byproduct of its maintenance, symbolic racism. As we have seen through our participants' shared stories, when they questioned authority it came with a cost. The cost often came in the form of "spotlight or racial image, anxiety" depicted by Cross (1991) or racial microaggressions described by Huber and Solorzano (2015). As our participants' stories show, they have found ways to resist and remain resilient, yet they are still subject to the impact of social dogma in the roles that they play or do not play within their own educational journeys. In many ways, this action is coupled with a form of inaction as well. Questions from this perspective arise that suggests that many of our students suffer from a double-victimization both educationally and consciously through the common practice of what Paulo Freire (2000) coined as the *banking model of education*. Unfortunately, most, due to social dogma, never truly question what is being deposited.

Final Remarks

It is well past time that one of the largest school districts in rural Nacogdoches County takes the initiative and comes to the realization of what the majority of African American/Black students' realities consists of. The message and issue that this chapter, and even this book conveys is not a new one. The issue at hand is one that has been entrenched in this community for several decades, and it is time for a positive change in the young lives of marginalized children in this community. It becomes critical to listen and to hear voices from the margins while acknowledging that these voices are heard through activism for social equity. In taking this position, traditional values may in fact become more inclusive to represent a resounding choir comprised of all stakeholders within the community. At the conclusion of one of the conversations with the participants, someone stated that *I have a Voice* and then someone else followed with *I have a voice, so listen!* We recognize this as a call to acknowledge, appreciate, and understand as we embrace voices of all tones and pitches. What would a community and school district be like that centralized the voices of the historically oppressed?

References

Appiah, K. A., & Gates, H. L. Jr. (Eds.). (2004). *Africana: Civil rights: An a-z reference of the movement that changed America*. Philadelphia, PA: Running Press.

Anderson, J. D. (1988). *The education of Blacks in the south*, 1860-1935. Chapel Hill, NC: The University of North Carolina Press.

Bell, D. (2005). White superiority in America: Its legal legacy, its economic crisis. In R. Delgado & J. Stefancic (Eds.), *The Derrick Bell reader* (pp. 27-32). New York, NY: New York University Press.

Bonner, F. A., II. (Ed.). *Building on resilience: Models and frameworks of Black male success across the p-20 pipeline*. Sterling, VA: Stylus Publishing, LLC.

Chapman, T. K. (2013). You can't erase race! Using CRT to explain the presence of race and racism in majority white suburban schools. *Discourse: Studies in the Cultural Politics of Education*, *34*(4), 611-627. http://dx.doi.org/10.1080/01596306.2013.822619

Cross, W. E., Jr. (1991). *Shades of Black: Diversity of African-American identity*. Philadelphia, PA: Temple University Press.

Delpit, L. (2006). *Other people's children: Cultural conflict in the classroom.* New York, NY: The New Press.

Delpit, L. (2013). *Multiplication is for White people: Raising expectations for other people's children.* New York, NY: The New Press.

De Walt, P. S. (2009). *First generation U.S.-born Africans and the expanded nigrescence theory: The stretching of a theory for a "different" African American experience at a predominantly White institution of higher education.* PhD dissertation, University of Colorado at Boulder, United States. Retrieved August 23, 2010, from Dissertations & Theses: Full Text. (Publication No. AAT 3366587)

Du Bois, W. E. B. (1979). B*lack reconstruction in America: An essay toward a history of the past which Black folk played in the attempt to reconstruct democracy in America,1860-1880 (9th, ed.).* New York, NY: Atheneum.

Du Bois, W. E. B. (2003). *The souls of Black folk.* New York, NY: Barnes & Noble Classics.

Fanon. F. (2008). *Black skin, white masks* (R. Philcox, Trans). New York, NY: Grove Press Inc.

Fabelo, T., Thompson, M. D., Plotkin, M., Carmichael, D., Marchbanks, M. P., & Booth, E. A. (2011, July). *Breaking schools' rules: A statewide study on how school discipline relates to students' success and juvenile justice involvement.* College Station, TX: The Public Policy Research Institute, Texas A&M University, Council of State Governments Justice Center.

Freire, P. (2000). *Pedagogy of the oppressed, (30th Anniversary edition).* New York, NY: Continuum International Publishing Group (Original work published 1970).

Fuentes A. (2014). The schoolhouse as a jailhouse. In A. J. Nocella II, P. Parmar, & D. Stovall (Eds.), *From education to incarceration: Dismantling the school-to-prison pipeline* (pp. 37-53). New York, NY: Peter Lang.

Gay, G. (2010). *Culturally responsive teaching: Theory, research & practice* (2nd ed.). New York, NY: Teachers College Press.

Hayman, R. L. Jr. (2000). *The smart culture: Society, intelligence, and law.* New York, NY: New York University Press.

Huber, L. P., & Solorzano, D. G. (2015). Racial microaggressions as a tool for critical race research. *Race ethnicity and education, 18*(3), 297-320. doi:10.1080/13613324.2014.994173

Jones, J. M. (1997). *Prejudice and racism* (2nd ed.). New York, NY: McGraw-Hill.

Koppelman, K. L., & Goodhart, R. L. (2011). *Understanding human differences: Multicultural education for a diverse America* (3rd ed.). Boston, MA: Allyn & Bacon.

Ladson-Billings, G. (2013). Critical race theory – what it is not! In M. Lynn & A. D. Dixson (Eds.), *Handbook of critical race theory in education* (pp. 34-47). New York, NY: Routledge.

Lemert, C., & Bhan, E. (Eds.) (1998). *The voices of Anna Julia Cooper: Including a voice from the south and other important essays, papers, and letters.* Lanham, MD: Rowman & Littlefield Publishers.

Leong N. (2013). Racial capitalism. *Harvard Law Review, 126*(8), 2153-2225.

Morgan, H. (1995). *Historical perspectives on the education of Black children.* Westport, CT: Praeger.

Perry, T., Steele, C., & Hilliard, A. S., III. (2003). *Young, gifted, and Black: Promoting high achievement among African-American students.* Boston, MA: Beacon Press.

Profit, W., Mino, I., & Pierce, C. (2000). Blacks, stress in. In G. Fink (Ed.). *Encyclopedia of stress* (pp. 324-330). San Diego, CA: Academic Press.

Sears, D. O. (1988). Symbolic racism. In P. A. Katz & D. A. Taylor (Eds.), *Eliminating racism: Profiles in controversy* (pp. 53-84). New York, NY: Plenum.

Sleeter, C. E., & Cornbleth, C. (2011). *Teaching with vision: Culturally responsive teaching in standards-based classrooms.* New York, NY: Teachers College Press.

Solorzano, D. (1998). Critical race theory, race and gender microaggressions, and the experiences of Chicana and Chicano scholars. *Qualitative Studies in Education, 11*(1), 121-136.

Steele, C. M. (2009). A threat in the air: How stereotypes shape intellectual identity and performance. In E. Taylor, D. Gillborn, & G. Ladson-Billings (Eds.), *Foundations of critical race theory in education* (pp. 163-189). New York, NY: Routledge.

Stovall, D. (2013). Mayoral control: Reform, whiteness, and critical analysis of neoliberal educational policy. In B. Picower & E. Mayorga (Eds.), *What's race got to do with it?: Understanding racism, neoliberalism, and educational reform* (pp. 45-58) New York, NY: Peter Lang.

Texas Education Agency. (2015). Texas academic performance report: 2014-2015 Texas Academic Performance Report [Data file]. Retrieved from https://rptsvr1.tea.texas.gov/perfreport/tapr/2015/srch.html?srch=D

Woodson, C. G. (2006). *The mis-education of the Negro.* San Diego, CA: The Book Tree.

Social Injustice in East Texas: A Social Work Perspective

By: Dr. Emmerentie Oliphant and David Mitchell

Introduction

Social workers in rural East Texas have many opportunities to advocate for social justice and equality for all people. In order to effectively advocate for change, it is important for social work practitioners and educators to understand the social injustices in rural areas such as East Texas. Social injustices including discrimination, racism, and violations of basic human rights can be seen in isolated areas of East Texas as well as in other rural areas across the nation. In addressing violations of basic human rights, social workers and other helping professionals should work from a strengths perspective. In addition, it is important to understand that social injustice is a systemic problem, impacting all levels of society. Discrimination against one person in a community can influence quality of life for the individual, family, and the larger community. For example, in social work practice it has been observed that a child's self-esteem, ability to grow, and development of trusting relationships with other people may be negatively impacted if a child has been bullied due to their racial background. According to the National Association of Social Workers (NASW) Code of Ethics (2008), social workers should act to prevent and eliminate domination, exploitation, and discrimination against any person. In order to act on and prevent similar forms of social injustice, professionals should understand the nature and use of a strengths perspective.

Based on knowledge and experience of social injustice both locally and internationally, the authors designed a study to explore social injustices against African–American community members in East Texas. Graduate social work students organized focus group interviews over a period of three years to explore social injustices in rural East Texas. Graduate students explored challenges, strengths, and realities experienced by African-American families in East Texas. The students identified guiding questions such as, "How do micro-aggressions manifest in everyday life?" to identify and describe current social injustices. The purpose of this research was to explore and describe examples of social injustice, discrimination, oppression, and racism amongst African-American families in East Texas. Initial objectives of the study included 1) the exploration of practices of social injustice in East Texas, 2) the description of strengths of African-American individuals and families to survive these social injustices, and 3) the development of practice guidelines for social workers to address social injustice in the East Texas community. The study allowed the researchers to listen to stories of people who are experiencing social injustices. By listening to their stories, we can learn how to build strategies toward change.

This chapter focuses on social injustice, and how social workers can use strengths and survival of individuals and families as part of the process of healing. We include information about the current perceptions on social injustices and provide strategies for helping professionals to advocate for social justice in East Texas.

The Need to Address Social Injustices from a Social Work Perspective

Social justice according to Pico, Schulz, Steele, Taha, & Torres-Hardwig (2014) referred to a fundamental valuing of fairness and equity in resources, rights and treatment for marginalized individuals, and groups of people who do not share equal power in society because of their immigration, racial, ethnic, age, socioeconomic, religious heritage, physical ability, or sexual orientation status groups. Social workers deal with social justice issues as it relates to the human rights and quality of life of all people, including those populations that are at risk of being discriminated against. Social injustice in rural areas is often observed in the disproportionality of social services, including problems with access to services for all people.

Social workers are guided by different international and national Codes of Ethics. These codes provide important information on how to treat people with respect and dignity within the context of equality. The NASW Code of Ethics (2008) emphasized the importance of understanding oppression and discrimination based on issues such as race, ethnicity, and nationality. This code of ethics identifies the foundation of social work's perspective namely the core values of social justice, dignity and worth of a person, and integrity. All of these values are the essence of addressing social injustices. Several authors in social work practice and education highlight the role of social workers in a rural context. Ginsberg (2005) mentioned that Black invisibility, powerlessness, racial attitude, prejudice, inequality, and marginalization are characteristics of some rural areas in the United States. The author mentioned that one cannot clearly determine the effect of one barrier from another. According to Avant (2014), "African Americans in rural communities have consistently been disadvantaged compared to urban areas and other ethnic groups living in rural areas" (p. 75). Avant acknowledged high poverty rates and limited opportunities and benefits.

One of the main purposes of social work is to address and enhance the social wellbeing of the individual, family, and community. Social workers use skills to advocate for populations who are at risk, specifically those experiencing behavioral problems. At risk populations include people who do not have adequate resources or access to services, are discriminated against, and/or are marginalized in the community. When people who are discriminated against also experience social problems such as behavioral health, HIV/AIDS and/or substance abuse, the person can be more at risk. In a study by Oliphant, Young, Amodei, Villela-Perez, Mammah, German, & Meissner (2015) the authors described issues of survival of African-American women who are HIV positive. African-American women in East Texas who participated in a research project funded by the United States Department of Health and Human Services (HRSA) reported being marginalized. They described being vulnerable and that they experience many challenges related to discrimination. Their vulnerability is not only because of the HIV status, but also due to the fact that they experience social injustices. The women reported that they experience challenges such as stigma, isolation, shame, poverty, unemployment, and rejection by the community. On the other hand, the women also shared that they have strengths, which enable them to survive the difficulties they face. With the support of family members and service providers, they are able to cope with their HIV positive status.

Social work incorporates social justice practices in organizations, institutions, and society to ensure that basic human rights are met without prejudice. In terms of current practices in East Texas, social workers often observe social injustice in practice. Though these injustices are not well published, the reality is that social injustice does exist. It is important that all helping professionals become aware of the challenges people are experiencing and how these challenges often result in social trauma. In order to enhance social wellbeing and quality of life, social workers must focus on advocating for populations at risk and engage in practices to advance social and economic justice. Burton et al. (2010) and Hardaway and McLoyd (2009) emphasized the importance to address social injustices in practice through advocacy and macro-level change interventions. These interventions can take many different forms. For example, social workers can create partnership networks to engage community members in discussions about social issues. Community forums can be used as a platform to share experiences about social trauma in a positive way. Specific task groups can be charged to identify discrimination and racism in schools and colleges and ultimately to offer solutions. It is also important to include content about discrimination, oppression, and social trauma in program curricula when preparing social workers for practice.

How do we specifically address these issues? The authors of the chapter are of the opinion that we need to develop a deeper understanding of how social injustices manifest. In addition, we need to ask those community members who experience these injustices to share solutions, rather than decide what solutions will be best according to our own perspectives. Ginsberg (2005,) stated that:

> Certainly the starting point is to recognize the existence of the barriers confronting all minorities, barriers that act to reduce their quality of life and life choices. Individuals on both sides of the racial divide need to re-examine their role in creating and maintaining poverty, discrimination, prejudice, powerlessness and White privilege as barriers to equality.
>
> (p. 422)

Social Injustices: African-American Individuals and Families in East Texas

In the past, social wellbeing of individuals and families were impacted by issues such as separation of family members and acts of violence against children. Over the past 200 years, families and individuals have been victim to acts of injustice. People from different walks of life contributed to the wealth of information collected to develop an understanding of social injustices in East Texas for this study. Participants included African-American community volunteers, students, ministers, teachers, and members from African-American societies such as the Black Cowboy Association. The diversity of people who shared their stories gave important voice to the community. It is obvious that we can learn more about injustices, people's perceptions about injustices, and discrimination—and the need to act against it—when we listen to people who have experienced it firsthand. The participants identified several important issues related to their experiences of which three are highlighted in this chapter: 1) a lack of understanding of people, culture, and wellbeing; 2) the role of faith in surviving discrimination; and 3) the importance of strengths.

Gaining experiential knowledge about social injustices, including reactions to discrimination and perceptions of possible change, is an important step in addressing social trauma. Participants reported being frustrated by "a lack of understanding history, spiritual life, motivation, and hope." A lack of understanding can be interpreted as "an unwillingness by the community to change social injustice practice." Also participants reported being frustrated by "the lack of understanding racial slurs, inappropriate remarks, and disrespectful language." One participant indicated that "keeping silent about problems" adds a barrier to understanding discrimination.

Faith is a way to survive and it became obvious that the respondents believe that it can help a person survive challenges. Specific narratives included that "faith is a way of living," believing in strengths and the ability to survive. One person took a strengths perspective against discrimination by stating, "…refusing that any injustices will not be allowed to destroy." One of the participants shared the following, "We coped by believing in our faith. The strong will survive." Another participant mentioned difficult situations, "we prayed and sung our way through it". One participant indicated that "the key word is love" when talking about strategies to address social injustice. Faith impacts resilience, attitudes, and perceptions and can influence resolutions to the problems related to social injustice and discrimination.

Faith is a strengths approach and a resource of resilience providing empowering opportunities for African-Americans. In addition, determination and humility can create a strategic effort in addressing social injustice and discrimination. Oliphant (2008) discussed the fact that African-American families have significant strengths to help them cope with the realities of social injustice. For example, spirituality, active participation in religious activities, and the strong bonds within family systems were identified as strengths.

Although data collected highlighted the negative impact of ongoing oppression, the impact of strengths as part of coping were evident. Social injustice manifests in overt and covert situations related to oppression and people find positive ways to cope with it. Some of the narratives highlight the impact of discrimination, "I was treated unfairly at my job because I am Black" and "… their mannerisms change when I am in line in a store." Participants reflected on the importance of education, perseverance, church involvement, spiritual leadership, multicultural social events, and job opportunities. When participants were asked how they deal with action of social injustice, they responded "I would ignore it", "I would not do anything", "God wants me to love", "I could call them out – to explain their behavior", "I will find out why…", and "I will talk about it".

In terms of education, some responses included "education makes a person", "helps them to succeed", and "I am thankful I have a degree." It is important to mention that many of the participants shared that they did not feel they were treated unfairly or that they experienced social injustice on an ongoing basis.

Action and Advocacy for Change

There are many efforts in the East Texas community to embrace difference, advocate for change, and fight social injustices. People from all backgrounds stand together to explore new ways of learning from each other and to build relationships. Below are some suggestions by the authors to address social injustices:

Partnerships

Social workers need to collaborate with local, national, and international agencies and higher education institutes to bring about change and to address social injustice. Inter- and transdisciplinary collaboration is extremely important in addressing all injustices. As part of these collaborations, social workers can contribute to a strong network to bring about change. Social workers can play an important role in building a knowledge base about how discrimination, oppression, and social injustices manifest in rural areas.

Participatory Action

Participatory action is a strategy through which people's experiences are at the forefront. As mentioned earlier in this chapter, it is important to listen to the voices of people and include those voices in our advocacy efforts. Advocacy, decision-making, problem-solving, and finding solutions should not be for people but instead should be in action with people. Participatory action refers to shared responsibility and ownership of the change needed in the community. Capacity is built through efforts of participatory action, ownership of change efforts, and the development of culturally-sensitive initiatives. It is important for rural communities such as those in East Texas to include all community members in formal and informal decision-making.

Becoming Aware of the Realities of Social Injustices

As indicated earlier, it is important to understand the dynamics and realities of social injustices as part of addressing and eradicating social injustices. Understanding is a process that includes the development of awareness and knowledge. Starting with the development of an awareness of the existence of social injustice, social workers can assist the community to become aware of incidents of discrimination, racism, and oppression. Social workers can guide the community to become open to difference by learning about cultural backgrounds in a systematic way. Social events that are inclusive and aimed to bring about change are important examples of systematic learning. It is also important for the social worker to become aware of social injustices and to self-reflect on their own set of beliefs impacting views of social justice.

Developing Ways to Build Knowledge of Realities of Social Injustices

It is important for the community to collect information about any form of discrimination, human rights violations, racism, and oppression and to make people aware of it. Many professionals, volunteers and community members fight social injustices and advocate for change. We can build knowledge about the resources to guide attitudes and behavior change, strategies to better understand the complexities of human rights violations, and the impact of culture on family and community relationships. By educating community members about the existence of these injustices, professionals can increase an awareness and sensitivity about it. Martin, Track, Peterson, Martin, Baldwin, & Knapp (2010) emphasized the importance of developing knowledge about cultural patterns of behavior and issues of fear and trust.

Education about Social Trauma

Ongoing education of people in terms of human rights and how it impacts society is necessary to empower those who experience social trauma. People need to be educated about the effect of trauma and how human right violations result in a loss of freedom, safety, and privacy. Education about values such as respect and dignity towards others must aim at building bridges in a community. Sellers and Shelton (2003) provided an overview of the major risk factors African-American individuals and families face including poverty and isolation imposed by scarcity, racism, and discrimination in the rural communities. Avant (2014) mentioned that "affective knowledge through which affect (feelings or emotions) is viewed as a valid source of knowing" (p. 79). By listening to people's experiences and sharing the information an effective education about how to advocate for change can be strengthened.

Using Strengths to Build Resilience

DiNotto and McNeese (2008) stated, "given the nature and culture of rural communities, social workers need to embrace a model that assumes that people already have ways to meet their needs" (p. 348). Such a model is strengths-based and operates on the premise that individuals and families who function at any level are functional. According to the authors, rural communities can benefit from natural helping networks, friends, religious groups, civic organizations, agricultural extension services and other organizations. Social support in rural areas is considered as strength in addressing discrimination and oppression.

The strengths perspective provides comprehensive principles to enable social workers, helping professionals, volunteers, and community members to empower the community rather than to have a community break down through the means of oppression. This perspective plays an important role in the development of effective strategies to advocate for change and to address human rights violations. Based on the fact that each individual has specific strengths, it is assumed that these strengths can be used as part of empowerment. The strengths perspective implies that individuals have strengths that enable them to be resilient.

Authors such as Saleebey, (2000), Burton, Bonilla-Silva, Ray, Buckelew, & Hordge-Freeman (2010) and Oliphant et al. (2015) emphasized the importance of focusing on strengths even in difficult situations. Even though it is important to use a problem-solving model to address problems, it is important to focus on strengths. The strengths perspective builds on positive relationships; the development of resources; resilience in individuals, families, groups and communities; and the competency to resolve problems in a positive way.

The strengths perspective is useful in advocating for change as it relates to social injustice. Strengths-based practice focuses on client strengths, rather than the problems. It aims to find solutions and positive attributes amidst the challenges of discrimination and social injustice. The departure point is that people have the inner strengths to survive challenges and difficulties in life. People's inner strengths enable them to cope with challenges and barriers in their everyday life situation. The inner strengths can be drawn from positive relationships, an active spiritual life, involvement in the community, strong sense of self, and significant partnerships in working with others. Although the strength perspective guides people to take care of their own life situations, this perspective also encourages community leaders, members, volunteers, and professionals to actively seek solutions for social trauma. Focusing on the strengths enables any person who experiences social trauma to learn and grow in a positive way. Although barriers and challenges should be acknowledged, it should not be the main focus in advocating for change.

A society that embraces social justice encourages diversity and equality, addresses all human rights, and encourages accessibility to a positive quality of life. This would be a safe place for all people to live work, relax, and grow. This society empowers people and develops strong assets in the community. The strengths perspective allows for people whose rights have been violated to reflect on their own ability to survive the difficulties they have experience. It allows for people to explore their strengths and to focus on solutions rather than problems.

Conclusion

Social workers and other human service professionals must prioritize their advocacy efforts for people who have experiences social trauma. All professionals addressing social trauma need to explore strategies to promote social justice for African-Americans in East Texas. While many different strategies exist, it is important to find which ones are most effective in a rural area. Strategies that are most effective are based on the strengths perspective. This implies that the focus of interventions should rather be on solutions than problems. Effective interventions should include advocacy and promotion of equality throughout the community. It is important to develop participatory action strategies and to engage persons who have experienced social trauma in all change efforts. Participatory action includes all stakeholders in discussions about social justice issues in the community. Spiritual and educational leaders should be invited to be part of all participatory action strategies. It allows for all people to voice their concerns in a positive and safe environment. The strengths perspective informs social work practice and builds on assets, solutions, and skills. Social workers and other human service providers can effectively integrate the strengths perspective as well as participatory action to address social injustice in rural East Texas.

References

Avant, F. L., Streeter, C. L., & Cooper, H. S. (2014). *Rural social work: Building and sustaining community capacity*. Hoboken, N.J.: Wiley.

Burton, L. M., Bonilla-Silva, E., Ray, V., Buckelew, R., & Hordge-Freeman, E. (2010). Critical race theories, colorism, and the decade's research on families of color. *Journal of Marriage and Family*, 72, 440-459.

Ginsberg, L. H. (2005). *Social work in rural communities* (4th Ed.). Washington D.C.: CSWE.

Hardaway, C. R., & McLoyd, V. C. (2009). Escaping poverty and securing middle class status: How race and socioeconomic status shape mobility prospects for African Americans during the transition to adulthood. *Journal of Youth and Adolescence*, 38, 242-256.

Martin, S. S., Track, J., Peterson, T., Martin, B. C., Baldwin, J., & Knapp, M. (2010). Influence of culture and discrimination on care-seeking behavior of elderly African American: A qualitative study. *Social Work in Public Health*, 25, 311-324.

Oliphant, E. (2008). *Proceedings from Bright Ideas Conference*. Stephen F. Austin State University. Nacogdoches, TX.

Oliphant, E., Young, N, Amodei, N., Villela-Perez, V, Mammah, R., German, V. F., & Meissner, P. (2015). The use of survival stories to empower HIV + women of color. *International Journal of Business, Humanities and Technology*, 5(3), 13–19.

Pico, C., Schulz, E., Steele,C., Taha, F., & Torres-Hardwig, S. (2014). Student perceptions of social justice and social justice perceptions. *Education, Citizenship and Social Justice*, 9(1), 69–76.

Saleebey, D. (2000). Power in the people: Strengths and hope. *Advances in Social Work*, 1, 127-136.

Confessing Whiteness

2 Corinthians 5: 16-21; Acts 10: 9-36 (*New Revised*, Standard Version)

By: Rev. Kyle Childress
Austin Heights Baptist Church, Nacogdoches, Texas

Since 1970, Austin Heights Baptist Church has had a partnership with Zion Hill First Baptist Church. The partnership began with the friendship between the two pastors of the churches, Reverend (Rev.) Jerry Self of Austin Heights and Rev. T.W. Berry of Zion Hill. The two congregations also were significantly involved in public education since both public school teachers and administrators as well as college teachers were members. Therefore, the two churches found themselves together working to desegregate the Nacogdoches schools in the early 1970s. The partnership began to bloom with joint worship services held twice a year --once in December at Zion Hill and once in April at Austin Heights -- with the visiting pastors preaching and the visiting choirs singing. The congregations would then share the Lord's Supper and following the service, a meal, which has become the subject of legends. Out of this partnership, have come various joint mission endeavors: work on Habitat houses, sharing work on the African-American Heritage Project, Vacation Bible School, etc.

This partnership, as well as friendships out of the joint fellowship, have helped the members of Austin Heights to see racism differently. With patient conversation with Zion Hill members, some of our blindness to our White privilege has begun to come into focus.

One Sunday night at Zion Hill, I thanked them and their pastor at the time, the late Rev. Larry D. Wade, for helping "de-White" our congregation and me. To "de-White" means that we've been going through a kind of White rehab for a long time. It doesn't mean we're trying to cease being White (which is impossible), and it does not mean that we're caught up in the guilt of being White. It simply means that we're learning to see differently and that we're becoming aware of White privilege, White transparency, and the White normativity of our society. The sermon, that follows was preached the following Sunday morning to the Austin Heights congregation.

This reading from Acts chapter 10 concerns seeing differently. The story begins with the Roman officer Cornelius having a vision of an angel telling him to send emissaries to Joppa to find Simon Peter. The next day, while the emissaries approach the city, Peter too has a vision. He sees heaven opened and a large sheet lowered containing all sorts of non-kosher animals and a voice saying to him, "Kill and eat… What God has made clean, you must not call profane."

Peter resisted this word three times, and three times the voice from heaven repeated the instructions. Peter resisted because Leviticus 11 tells faithful Jews what is lawful to eat and what is not, what is kosher and what is not. This is about being a Jew and it's about reading the Bible. How to eat and what to eat and not eat was and is part of the very identity of being a Jew. It is not optional or an addendum. It is the faith. It is a commandment of God, and it was something Peter had learned from birth so that by his adulthood it was who he was.

So do you see why he resisted this vision? He's being asked to go against everything he knew to be right, good, and godly. He's being asked to go against the Bible, and he is being asked to go against his very identity and the identity of the people of God.

This story from Acts can help us get a handle on being "White." The kind of Whiteness I'm talking about is a way of seeing which is so pervasive in our culture that we don't even notice it. Indeed, one of the characteristics of Whiteness is that it is considered to be so normal (White normativity) that we don't know we're participating (White transparency) in something that developed in early modern times. Whiteness and the concept of race is something that came along with the colonialism of the seventeenth, eighteenth, and nineteenth centuries. Race or Whiteness is not just about ethnicity; it is about structured systems of power where lighter skins are higher up on the hierarchy. Being White was considered to be better, more evolved, more developed, more civilized, and therefore it justified that White people were meant to rule, conquer, and colonize (White privilege).

We say that we don't believe that anymore, but what we fail to do is realize how much of that old way is still the way our world operates. That old way I'm referring to is called racism. Most of us White people tend to focus upon the overt racial prejudices of the individual person and call that racism. We tend to think that simple education can change the individual and therefore change racism. We also tend to think that Black people or Brown people also have their own prejudices (and they do) and therefore they are racists too – which is not correct.

Racism is not simply about an individual having racial prejudices. Racism – and this is important – is about prejudice combined with power. Racism is systemic. It is the air we breathe so that we don't notice it – if we are White. It is systemic power and privilege which assumes the norm for the good, the true, and the beautiful is determined by Whiteness. It is so normal that we assume that it is the way the world is supposed to be and the way God wants it to be. If the air that we breathe results in lung cancer we get an idea of the invisible power of what we breathe. Likewise, racism, the power of Whiteness, results in inequality, injustice, poverty, and on and on.

May I make a suggestion? For the next two days anytime you refer to someone who is White, preface it with the word "White." If you refer to me in a conversation, say, "My White pastor, Rev. Childress." If you refer to your teacher, say something like, "My White teacher." When speaking about your friend, refer to them as "my White friend." Those of you who are Black will most likely not think speaking like this is odd. It is not uncommon for you to refer to people by their racial group.

But for those of us who are White, people who will hear you will likely think you're odd. White is the imagined norm of identity in the United States. As the norm, it needs no modifier. Those of us who are White will likely feel odd referring to everyone who is White with the modifier "White." We will also likely think it is wrong. But this simple exercise should not be a big deal; it's not wrong and it's not racism. It is simply an exercise that reminds us being

White is transparent or invisible to those of us who are White.

Ask yourself, "What do you like about being White?" For most of us, we'll have to think about that for a while because it is not something we've thought about before. Whiteness is just who we are and the way it is. We don't have to think about it. It's kind of like asking a fish in the ocean what it's like to swim in the water.

Not so with Blackness. A century ago, W. E. B. Du Bois asked the question of his fellow Blacks, "How does it feel to be a problem?" For us Whites, we've never had to ask what it feels like to be a problem.

Back to our story with Peter in Acts 10 – in the Bible people were aware of different colors of skin and different ethnic groups or "nations" as it is sometimes translated. But the notion that White-skinned people were what was normal and any other color of skin was abnormal, and that the White and lighter skin tones were superior to others is not something in the Bible. It came along after the Bible. Years ago I lived in Atlanta, Georgia, in a predominately Black neighborhood. When I needed to do my laundry, I walked down the street to a laundromat that was next door to a little café that sold soul food and next door to a record store, which did not have any Barry Manilow or Doobie Brothers. I was always the only White person in the laundromat. All the neighbors were Black. And when I ventured further out in the city, there was a much higher percentage of Black people everywhere than what I had known in small-town west Texas, or where I had grown up or in Waco, or where I went to Baylor. In Atlanta, I was aware of being White in a mostly Black context and in places like the laundromat I was somewhat uncomfortable. Yet over time, I became friends with some of the neighbors, and eventually quit noticing it. I didn't realize how much I had changed until I flew home for Christmas. I distinctly remember getting off the plane in the Dallas/Fort Worth airport and walking out into the terminal and saying to myself, "Wow! Look at all the White people."

What happened is that for the first time my eyes had been opened to my "Whiteness," and I began to see differently. I was beginning to be "de-Whited."

To be de-Whited, to confess our Whiteness, does not mean to wring our hands or go around feeling guilty. It means having our vision changed. It means opening our eyes to privilege and power and assumptions that we never noticed before. And when we do that, we can begin to change our behavior and we can begin to address our racialized society.

In our Scripture reading from II Corinthians 5, the Apostle Paul says, "From now on, therefore, we regard no one from a human point of view; even though we once knew Christ from a human point of view, we know him no longer in that way. So if anyone is in Christ, there is a new creation: everything old has passed away; see, everything has become new!" (2 Cor. 5: 16-17). The call is not to become colorblind. Indeed, we are called to cease being blind to what color means in our society. We want our eyes opened, not closed. But we want to learn to see differently; to see from the perspective of Christ where we can see ruthfully.

This is what happened to Peter in Acts 10. He began the journey, the process of seeing in and through Christ instead of seeing from a human point of view. The story says that when the emissaries from the Roman officer and Gentile Cornelius showed up where Peter was staying and practicing hospitality, the emissaries were invited in. Eventually, Peter goes back with them to Cornelius's house in Caesarea Maritima, the headquarters for Rome in Judea.

Upon arriving, he is received in hospitality. He hears of Cornelius's vision and briefly explains his own vision, which has begun to teach him to see in Christ. Peter says, "I truly understand that God shows no partiality." And he begins to preach and teach the gospel of Christ to the entire household. As a result, the Holy Spirit of God comes upon the entire gathering, and in turn, everyone is baptized.

Baptism means many things, but chief among them is that in baptism we enter into the new people of God. Paul told the Galatians, "As many of you as were baptized into Christ have clothed yourselves with Christ. There is no longer Jew or Greek, there is no longer slave or free, there is no longer male and female; for all of you are one in Christ Jesus" (Galatians, 3: 27-28).

We become members of this body of Christ, this new people, and our sisters and brothers sit next to us, sit across from us and down from us every Sunday morning. But we Austin Heights folks have been learning for nearly fifty years that it also means that we are one with Purcell and Dorothy Warren, Mr. and Mrs. Burrell, Mrs. Wade, Hugh and Anedra Perkins, and with all those who go by the name Zion Hill First Baptist Church.

Over time, we learn that we want to hear their stories, sing their songs, and learn to see as they do. We want to do that because we long to have a deeper relationship with Jesus Christ; part of what that means is that we are to have a deeper relationship with our fellow members of the body of Christ. We learn that to participate in one another is to participate in Christ. When we practice hospitality in receiving one another in December and April, as in Acts 10, we are receiving Jesus. We gather around the Lord's Table, sing hymns and spirituals, and then enjoy a feast together; we are beginning to practice what God intends for all of us every day.

Paul says, "All this is from God, who reconciled us to himself through Christ, and has given us the ministry of reconciliation" (2 Corinthians, 5: 18).

When I left Atlanta to move to Louisville, Kentucky, I asked a veteran Black pastor and veteran activist of the Civil Rights Movement what I needed to do to help be a reconciler across racial lines when I became a pastor. He told me to join Black groups and organizations in town, to volunteer and work, to be intentional and get involved, but be quiet and listen. Don't make suggestions; don't organize or seek to be in charge. Just listen and learn and serve. In other words, give up control and assumptions about leadership. Just listen. Just learn.

Part of being de-Whited is to listen and learn and give up our assumptions. One of the most powerful ways we can begin to do that is to allow our suffering, our pain and our grief to become a place of contact with the Black church. The Black church, its preaching, its worship, and especially its music has been about taking its hurt, grief, and suffering and seeing it through the hurt, grief, and suffering of Jesus. In so doing, the suffering is transformed; hope is born anew, and the church is empowered to keep on. When we are in touch with our own suffering, and learn to lift it up in Christ through the spirituals of the Black church, besides our own healing and hope, we find ourselves being drawn closer to our sisters and brothers who are Black.

Being de-Whited is also learning to hear of the injustice suffered by our Black sisters and brothers and then be willing to walk alongside of them. To hear of the fear of being pulled over by the police when you know that you have not done anything wrong. To hear of the fear of being in a neighborhood in which violence is on the streets yet the fear is compounded by the fear of calling the police. To hear what it feels like as a professor with a Ph.D., to walk into a store and have a store clerk follow you around keeping an eye on you. To hear what it's like to have so many of the young men of your neighborhood in prison or unemployed or dropping out of school. To hear how African-American boys are taught to carry their wallet and ID in their front pockets, so when stopped by the police, they will not have to reach back to get their ID for fear of being shot. To hear of the despair, the lack of hope in so many Black lives and Black families.

We have to be intentional, and we have to listen and learn from our sisters and brothers who are Black. This takes time and togetherness. It means giving up our assumptions.

An old African proverb says, "To go fast, walk alone. To go far, walk together." We cannot heal racism by going fast or going alone. We cannot be a whole community by getting in a hurry and trying to give it a quick fix. This is long-haul kind of stuff. We can only do it together with friends, with sisters and brothers who are black and who remind us of our Whiteness.

Contributors

Editor Bios

DAWN MICHELLE WILLIAMS taught special education for 20 years, served 10 years as a middle and high school administrator in Kansas and Texas, and is currently employed as an associate professor and coordinator of the middle level grade online completer program at Stephen F. Austin State University in the Department of Elementary Education. She holds Masters Degrees in Special Education and Educational Administration, and completed her Doctorate in Educational Leadership at Stephen F. Austin State University.

BRANDON L. FOX has been an Assistant Professor in the Department of Elementary Education at Stephen F. Austin State University since 2012. He received his doctorate from Texas A&M University in 2011 and his bachelor's degree (2005) and master's degree (2008) from Stephen F. Austin State University.

Author Bios

JERRY WILLIAMS is a Professor of Sociology at Stephen F. Austin State University in Nacogdoches, Texas where he teaches a variety of courses including race and ethnic relations. He holds a bachelor's degree from Eastern Oregon University and a master's and Ph. D. from Kansas State University. His research focuses upon phenomenology and the human relationship to the environment. His publications include sociological articles, philosophical essays, a monograph, edited books, and poetry.

ROLONDA TEAL is an ethnographer who has worked extensively in Louisiana with various cultural groups. In 2007 she published "African Americans in Natchitoches Parish" - a photographic essay that covers the lives of local residents from the antebellum period to the Civil Rights Era. Teal has also contributed to the American Anthropology Association's online publication, Racism in the Academy in 2012.

Teal's work with the Underground Railroad led to the first connection in the country that ties a National Historic Trail with an established enslaved escape route. Ms. Teal is currently a Ph.D. student at Stephen F. Austin State University where she is pursuing a degree in Forestry with a concentration in Human Dimensions.

TOM MIDDLEBROOK has practiced Child and Adolescent Psychiatry in Nacogdoches since 1988. He is a native of Nacogdoches and has family roots here since the early 1820's. He received his B.S. (cum laud, Geology, 1977) and M.A. (Psychology, 1977) degrees from Stephen F. Austin State University. Additionally, he holds a D.C.S. (Theology, 1977) degree from Regent College in Vancouver, BC, Canada and a MD (1983) degree from Southwestern Medical School (University of Texas Health Science Center at Dallas).

Tom has been interested in East Texas heritage since childhood. He first visited and participated in an archeological dig during the Lake Nacogdoches excavations of 1975. He has since served as Presidents of the Dallas Archeological Society, the East Texas Archeological Society and the Texas Archeological Society. For over twenty-five years he has been a Steward of the Texas Archeological Stewardship Network of the Texas Historical Commission.

He is a Past-Chairman of the Nacogdoches County Historical Commission. In 2015, Tom received the Donald T. Crabtree Award from the Society for American Archaeology for his outstanding avocational contributions in "advancing archeology through research, fieldwork, education, and public outreach."

Tom's other interests include astronomy, history, backpacking, growing roses and cooking. He is married to Sylvia Middlebrook, PhD, Asst. Professor of Psychology at Stephen F. Austin State University. He has five children and seven grandchildren.

DIANNE DENTICE is an Associate Professor of Sociology at Stephen F. Austin State University. She received her Ph.D. in Sociology from Texas Women's University in 2006. From 2005 through 2012 she conducted field research with various Klan and neo-Nazi groups in Texas, Arkansas, and Louisiana, and Mississippi. She has published numerous scholarly studies that deal with that research. She teaches classes in race and ethnic relations, social problems, gender, marriage and family, and social psychology.

ROBERT F. SZAFRAN is a Regents Professor of Sociology at Stephen F. Austin State University. He teaches courses in demography and research methods and publishes in the areas of social indicators, research design, and computer simulation. His PhD in Sociology is from The University of Wisconsin at Madison.

OSARO AIREN currently serves as the Dean of Student Retention at Cedar Valley College. He previously served as the Director of Multicultural Affairs and Graduate Faculty at Stephen F. Austin State University. He received a Bachelor of Arts in Psychology from the University of California, Riverside (UCR), a Master of Marriage and Family Therapy from the University of Southern California (USC), a Master of Business Administration (MBA) from Wayne State College, and a Ph.D. in Counselor Education from Virginia Tech. He is also a Licensed Professional Counselor (LPC), National Certified Counselor (NCC), and Certified Disaster Support Counselor.

JUSTIN IKPO is a graduate of Stephen F. Austin State University. He receieved his bachelor's degree journalism and secondary education in 2013. He currently works in marketing for The College of Education and Human Development at Texas A&M University. He previously worked for Nacogdoches Independent School District, where he did public relations work. It was during this time that he became heavily involved in the diverse and unique community of Nacogdoches, representing both parents and students. It proved to be a welcoming aspect of his career as he drew experiences from his own upbringing in the inner city of Houston.

KIMBERLY FOLI is a graduate of East Tennessee State University, where she received a bachelor's degree in journalism in 2010. She now works in marketing at Texas A&M university. Prior to working at the university, she was a reporter and news editor at The Daily Sentinel in Nacogdoches. It was during this time that she met and interviewed many members of the African-American community who were willing to candidly discuss the past and present condition of race relations in East Texas.

ALISHA HALL is a 2005 Stephen F. Austin State University graduate. She received a Bachelor of Arts in Public Administration.

VERDIS DANIELS, JR. was born January 1, 1959 in Lufkin, Tx. He is the second oldest of seven children raised by his mother in Nacogdoches, Texas. He graduated from Nacogdoches High School in 1977 and joined the US Air Force, serving 7 years at Bergstrom AFB. Verdis attended Austin Community College, worked for the Internal Revenue Service and currently for the State of Texas. He lives in Austin, Texas has three children: Don D. Carter, Cherita M. Daniels, both of Austin, and Margaret L Daniels of Stone Mountain, Ga.

BROOKE LA'SHUN TAYLOR-JOHNSON is a born-native of Nacogdoches, Texas where she is currently a senior at Stephen F. Austin State University studying Interdisciplinary Studies, Elementary Education concentrating on pre-kindergarten through sixth grade. Taylor-Johnson attended Nacogdoches Independent School District her entire elementary and secondary educational career.

PATRICK S. DE WALT (Ph.D., University of Colorado at Boulder) is an Assistant Professor in the Department of Elementary Education in the James I. Perkins College of Education at Stephen F. Austin State University. Dr. De Walt's research interests include racial and cultural identity with an emphasis on the African Diaspora, teacher education and issues of diversity, curriculum development through the incorporation of digital media, and theory and pedagogy. Dr. De Walt earned a B.S. in Biology from Prairie View A&M University, an M.Ed. in Curriculum & Instruction/Elementary Education from the University of Houston, an M.B.A. in General Business from the University of Houston-Victoria. Before pursuing his terminal degree, Dr. De Walt taught within the Houston Independent School District as a first grade teacher. Each of these areas and experiences allows for an interdisciplinary approach to research as well as teaching and learning.

EMMERENTIE OLIPHANT is Professor and Director of the MSW Program, School of Social Work (Stephen F. Austin State University). She worked as a social worker and educator in South Africa since 1988 and joined SFA in 2006. While teaching at the University of Johannesburg in South Africa she was the project leader for several community development and family empowerment projects in the country. She worked as a consultant for agencies in South Africa on juvenile offender issues, social advocacy, restorative justice, HIV/AIDS, and substance abuse. In addition to teaching, she had a private practice in family counseling for 15 years. Dr. Oliphant is a council member of the CSWE Council for Practice and Specialized Methods in the US and a board member for the Texas Evaluation Network (TEN). She is actively involved in the East Texas community. She serves on the Nacogdoches Area United Executive Board of Directors, works closely with San Augustine County to assess their needs and enhance service delivery, and is one of the principal investigators for a HRSA funded HIV/AIDS project in Tyler and Longview. Emmerentie is currently the principal investigator of the Impact Lufkin community empowerment project funded by the T.L.L. Temple Foundation.

DAVID MITCHELL, MSW lives in Longview, Texas and he works as a clinical mental health provider in Shreveport, Louisiana. Mr. Mitchell is a Post-Vietnam era veteran that served in the U. S. Army. He lived as a San Francisco Bay Area resident during the Flower Power, Hippie, Black Panther movements, and Angela Davis trial. As a Texas resident, in the 1960s he has experienced a segregated South under Jim Crow laws. He is a graduate of Stephen F. Austin State University with a Master's and a Bachelor's degree in social work. He has an Associate of Arts from Kilgore College. He is also a Longview High School (Lobos) graduate. He is a member of Who's Who in American Colleges and Universities, Phi Theta Kappa, Phi Alpha, Sigma Kappa Delta.

KYLE CHILDRESS has served as the pastor of the Austin Heights Baptist Church in Nacogdoches, Texas since 1989. A graduate of Baylor University with a Bachelor of Arts in Religion and History, Southern Baptist Theological Seminary with a Master of Divinity and with post-graduate work at the Duke University Divinity School, Kyle is the author of over fifty published articles and has contributed chapters in five books. He was guest lecturer and preacher in 2008 at the 200th anniversary of Andover Newton Theological Seminary in Boston as part of their Great Preaching Series and has delivered lectures at Baylor University's Truett Seminary, Duke Divinity School, Baptist Theological Seminary of Richmond, Virginia, and the Associated Biblical Mennonite Seminary in Elkhart, Indiana. Kyle is married to Jane, a poet and they have two adult daughters, Emily and Callie.

www.ingramcontent.com/pod-product-compliance
Lightning Source LLC
Chambersburg PA
CBHW061150070526
44584CB00034B/4471